We Are One:

POEMS FROM THE PANDEMIC

T0349269

We Are One:

POEMS FROM THE PANDEMIC

Edited by

George Melnyk

BAYEUX ARTS
DIGITAL-TRADITIONAL PUBLISHING

WE ARE ONE: Poems from the Pandemic

Copyright (c) George Melnyk 2020

Publication: October 2020

Published in Canada by
Bayeux Arts, Inc.
2403, 510 – 6th Avenue, S.E.
Calgary, Canada T2G 1L7

www.bayeux.com

Cover Design: Munaf Husain

'On a walk through a park, you stop for a moment, and you look above...
And you are transfixed.
As I continued walking I remember wondering - why does nature's poetry reveal itself to you at certain times, while at others you simply walk right past it?'
--MUNAF HUSAIN

Book design by Lumina Datamatics

Library and Archives Canada Cataloguing in Publication

Title: **We are One: Poems from the Pandemic / edited by George Melnyk.**
Other titles: **We are One (Bayeux)**
Names: **Melnyk, George, editor.**
Identifiers: **Canadiana (print) 20200286706 | Canadiana (ebook) 20200286889 | ISBN 9781988440484 (softcover) | ISBN 9781988440491 (EPUB)**
Subjects: **LCSH: COVID-19 (Disease)—Poetry. | LCSH: Epidemics—Poetry. | LCSH: Canadian poetry—21st century. | CSH: Canadian poetry (English)—21st century.**
Classification: **LCC PS8287.C68 W4 2020 | DDC C811/.60803561—dc23**

The ongoing publishing activities of Bayeux Arts Digital - Traditional Publishing under its varied imprints are supported by the Government of Alberta, Alberta Multimedia Development Fund, and the Government of Canada through the Book Publishing Industry Development Program.

Printed in Canada

This book is dedicated to all those who sacrificed their lives
to save the lives of those with COVID-19

Table of Contents

Editor's Foreword

Dr. Ashis Gupta, novelist, poet, and publisher of Bayeux Arts conceived this book in the spring of 2020 and he invited me to serve as the book's editor by soliciting poems for this anthology and then selecting them for publication. Earlier he had published two similar poetry anthologies commemorating natural catastrophes and disasters. He believed that the COVID-19 pandemic deserved a similar response.

The title of this collection, *We Are One: Poems from the Pandemic* expresses the solidarity that we have with those who suffered and died through the first wave of the Covid-19 pandemic in Canada. This includes the seniors who became vulnerable due to public and private mismanagement; it includes those separated from loved ones by isolation and quarantine; and it includes each and every person, young and old, who struggled with the impact of social distancing and constant online communication. The poets in this anthology capture the emotional impact of a new way of living the contemporary world had never before experienced.

My criteria for selection was multi-faceted. The anthology was built around geographic representation, diversity in style, inclusiveness, and thematic relevance. I wanted to capture the fullest range possible of pandemic experiences in Canada (and some from abroad) by as diverse a body of poets as possible in the short time I had to put the manuscript together. This book contains poems of great sophistication and it also contains doggerel. I felt that only by incorporating the brilliant and the humdrum and everything in between could the vast array of experiences related to the pandemic be authentically captured. Themes of love and grief, of travel and quarantine, of isolation and physical distancing, and the myriad of other traumas and mental adjustments that so many of us had to make became the focus of the book. In these poems I hope readers will see something of their own experiences, whether negative or positive.

Established poets and emerging poets vied for a place in the anthology and I approached each submission with an open mind. Over 150 poets submitted 285 poems. The limit was three per person. Keeping track of the large volume of submissions was aided greatly by a spreadsheet developed by my wife, Julia Berry Melnyk. Her conceptualization of data retention kept me grounded and unflustered during the submission process. She also contributed to the selection process with her insights. I offered her a co-editorship, which she rightly deserved, but in her modesty she said no. I couldn't have done this project without her assistance. I am also grateful to Bob Stallworthy, Monty Reid, Ivan Sundal, Jane Ross, Weyman Chan, Alice Major, Harry Thurston, Mary Dalton, Myrna Kostash, Colin Morton, Micheline Maylor, Roberta Rees, Richard Harrison, and Rhea Tregebov for circulating the news of the book among their poetry colleagues or providing me with contacts. I also want to thank Lesley Fletcher, Executive Director of the League of Canadian Poets for sending out a call for submissions to the League's members on my behalf. Practically all of the poems are previously unpublished. I have included poems by municipal poet laureates who were commissioned to write a poem on the pandemic as part of their official duties. I consider them a valuable addition to this volume.

This volume that spans the country, touches on numerous themes and common experiences associated with the pandemic in 2020, and expresses a wide range of emotional responses to the suffering, both economic and social, that millions underwent and are still dealing with. The power of poetry to memorialize, to sustain, to question, to bring tears and even laughter to traumatic situations is something this book celebrates. It is meant to make you cry and laugh and remember sadness, the bizarre and the heartwarming. I am grateful to every poet that submitted work for consideration because each poem represented a voice engaged with a world of restrictions, distancing, anxiety, and fear of being near even those we love. The poems celebrate the caring, the humour, and inventiveness of human beings facing daunting challenges.

I hope these poems will remind you of what we faced in the spring and summer of 2020. May they express in some small way what you felt and, more importantly, what you did to survive. These poems are a tribute to you.

George Melnyk

Calgary

Family

Sarah Ens

This New Spring

In this new spring,
my grandmother
learns FaceTime,
pours milky eyes
into the care home's
shared screen. An aide
holds it to her
like some kind of proof.
My grandmother
this past winter whispered
into clasped hands:
I was never homesick
when I was with Abe—

Abe my grandfather, who,
when he passed, unmoored
her, and we
had to pin the funeral
program above her sink
so she'd remember.
His strong body resisted
death. For months,
he wrenched restraints
at his wrists.

This new spring,
the sun is always waning,
the wind is a weapon, and the river
flocks with shorebirds
jolting silver to sky.
For so many springs

my grandmother's hands
would swirl soapy water
or, webbed with dough,
shape rows of *tweebakje*
to softly rise. At the table
beside my grandfather,
she'd interlock her fingers
with his in prayer.

In this new spring,
children spread
quilts on their separate
front lawns, purple-yellow
squares swathing muted grass,
and they stay safe,
read aloud across the street,
stand, sometimes, for volume.
Sidewalk chalk
reminds us to *take care*
of each other and the elms
shake their fists,
still alive.

I turn my phone to show
my grandmother
the chalk, the children,
muddy snow receding
to curbs, and branches bending
gnarled fingers to concrete.
She doesn't ask why
I don't visit. Instead:
Have the trees started yet
to green? This yearly miracle
safe in her memory,
renewing her faith
in each new spring.

John B Lee

Sometimes it's the Rain that Puts the Fire Out

in the midst
of this damned pandemic
I say
to my sorrowful son on the phone
who is sitting alone
in distant suburban darkness
his voice a lamentation
come from far away
in the needfulness of night
not knowing quite what I mean
I say …

"sometimes it's the rain
that puts the fire out …"

to think of the weather
come cooling in ash
with a hissing of cinders
grown heavy and damp
a dimming of embers
a fading of light
that glows into grey
so the fever goes out
of the oak

yet what a relief to the forest
that's elsewhere been leveled
by flame
to know where the boreal body remains
in one green breath

and I hear
his dog giving comfort
lapping with the noble thirst
of all beautiful creatures
his water song
slaking us all
with the contrapuntal splashing
of his long pink tongue
as with the labour
of a mournful sigh
both my grieving son and I
listen as an evening rain begins
to mend its way
across the lawn
this rain
that puts the fire out
this rain that comes to quench us both in healing tears

Vivian Hansen

Making a Man

Sometime during lockdown,
my grandson's voice changed.

He sent his rainy-day Instagram message,
but I couldn't hear him
as his mother took a sideview picture
of him staring out the living room window, clutching
a cup of coffee.

He wrote beneath his picture: *Absolutely no one,*
heeps and heeps o nobody,
me on a rainy morning.

His voice must have changed just then-
from an almost-there hastening that I heard in January,
into the depths of his June baritone.

Was it the pandemic lockdown that stole the moment from me?
Or maybe the delicate curve of his Adam's apple
desired to sleep securely beneath his chin
until the snow evaporated.

When I met him at the door in June,
we were both ready for a long hike on Nose Hill.
His first words to me as a man, approved
the vegetarian items in my picnic basket:
kimchi, spinach spanakopita, Babybel cheese
as round as his teenage mouth.

Four years earlier, I climbed Nose Hill with him to the glacial erratic,
aided by my diamond willow walking-stick.
A brown diamond hollow for the pressure of my thumb.
His starling boy-legs loped
upward, he didn't wait
for his aging grandmother.

Instead, he stalked each yellow buffalo bean,
pressed grey sage between his fingertips, sniffed.
saluted the tiny flags of butterflies.

Today I expect him to climb and reclimb
all the footholds and clefts on that erratic.
How he tried as a boy, to reach a sitting spot carved
by wind, just for him.
He reaches it easily now.
The past four years have carved him
much like this glacial stone,
with the storms of his father's cancer.

He has slowed, like a man. His new voice lauds
the hill around him, as he spies the city.
A small soft beard clings to his chin
like lichen against rock.

Like a man, he marks me before I even speak a word.
He prompts me for answers, to questions new and ancient.
I'd like to breathe truth into his eyes,
but his knowing will retrieve my DNA gently.

Today, after three months of lockdown,
his deep voice heralds tree roots before me.
He watches my steps, plotting the path.

Hiking behind me in the way of a man
who would practice a guarded step
for a woman he loves.

Myrna Garanis

My cousins have been in touch

one by one, checking in with the eldest.
We're distant kin by mileage, not design.
Once we numbered thirty-six, four passed
too young, cancer nipping at all our heels.

My cousins need to know I'm still kicking,
hence the e-mail flurry at this suddenly
significant moment, not waiting for the
usual Christmas reassurance, admitting,
in our sometimes jokey online ways,
that we are still connected. Warm body
counts, you could say.

My mother devoted hours writing three-
page letters to her siblings, nieces, nephews,
one of a kind for all occasions, used lined
stationery, her penmanship exemplary.
My own missives below her standards,

though I too favour pen 'n ink, mail
negatives instead of scanning. As eldest
and only child to boot, my duty to my
cousins is to hang in a little longer, allow
the family genes to keep us entwined.

Dennis Cooley

covid contact

house-pent she yearns for a mango sun
that would touch the yard into heat
wrap it in a pentecostal flare

she hopes for the birds that would
darn the light into nests
the tango of grass and earthworms

she quickens like a child to the excitement
her ipad lighting up the internet
with hints of contact and candour
when it dings quickquick like an ice-cream vendor
she also rouses to it like a slightly older kid to
a pinball machine in full tilt that may be
at any moment shaken into silence

the spasms of eight friends
) is anybody there . . . is anybody listening. . . (
could be SOS if they knew morse code
they cannot speak often or quickly enough
the eight of them at the same time
signal back, all at once, and once again, it seems
in boolean loop listing badly on a ship
the distress signals sounding the alarm

she grows so impossibly restive

the two daughters keep a fierce eye on her

they suspect her of a dangerously skittish bent

pawing and snorting around the gate

through which they fear she is apt to burst

like a cow newly sprung

from a long cold winter in the barn

hoping to acquire a herd immunity

Tea Gerbeza

Private Joys

I fold three-day-old laundry
into wrinkly parcels,
pack them away in wood
drawers. A red top
my mother lent me, stained
from the mud I slipped in last spring.

I want to send her the shirt:
a private joke she can hold
as she tries to garden,
hands in the earth, hoping
to feel something good.

I want to make *sarma,* hear her
scold, *you're adding too much salt!*
Hear Dad say I need to *chill down*
after I work myself up
over some character
in a television show.

My iPhone chimes
with selfies from Dad,
his German Shepherd puppy
nuzzles his neck, licks his smile,
chews his hair.

Will I see them again?

    Dread grows its own ventricle.
        Each new active case
            makes it harder to breathe.
                I squeeze the red blouse.

                The space becomes the world.

      I—

Matt brings a glass of water
and chocolate Mini-Eggs.
I drew you a bath.
He hands me a sketch
of a little claw-foot boat
bobbing down a stream of letters.

I don't understand the joke.
Underwater, I promise
to call my parents tomorrow,
listen to our apartment, deep
with Matt's laugh.

Joan Crate

Feb. 28, 2020: (for Kamal)

Head thrown back, sprawled across the bed
you are already dream and fallen flesh
travelling between worlds. One finger

on consciousness, you backstroke through
a Mid-Eastern childhood fractured by bombs,
your closest brother blown to bits, earth split
with drought and that river of years
that swept away a boy with a tapeworm.

In Canada's cold-throttled winter,
you were a non-entity with frost-bitten fingers
and a second-hand ski jacket haunting
Toronto streets, a young man barely seen,
hardly noticed.

> *How our acquisitions*
> *and projected identities*
> *collapse as we age*
> *into ourselves.*

          I watch your eyes shift
under closed lids, moving along currents
of time, your skin cool as fallen leaves while
your pulse races through an obstacle course
of disease.

         Moisture freezes on window glass.

I am on one side of the pane
and you on the other

         floating away from me.

Joan Crate

You are ashes and memory now

a sealed marble urn I pass by every morning,
stumbling to the kitchen for coffee.

We're in quarantine together: your charred
remains and my scattered grey thoughts.

There's no news on the TV other than the pandemic,
but yesterday I heard brakes squeal and metal crunch.

Today I awoke with road rash down my legs and glass
imbedded in my palms, screaming like a siren.

All day clouds and scavenger leaves
press against the bedroom window

mouthing your name.

Nature

Louise B. Halfe - Sky Dancer

Emerge

The sun's rays illuminate through the crocus's feathery petals
Having laid dormant for months in the deep darkness of the earth
Its unfolding emerges, stretches, and expands its wholeness.
Each morning after the slumber of sleep
Unaware of the haven of life without light we too rest.
Once in infancy we curled orbiting in the wet womb
We too, stretched, opened our mouths
Soul, life and wind emerged.
We've journeyed through these months of darkness
Limbs, mind, soul and body a little bruised and battered.
Sitting in the darkened sweat-lodge
The backbones of the Grandfather Rock glow
With the fire within. Water is sprinkled
The cloud's vapor drenches the skin.
This gestation and germination occurring
With the sweat-lodge is mere moments of darkness,
At birth labor is fifteen, twenty-eight hours
Through the uterine passage. To endure, persevere
In the gathering of the self we will be bruised, battered
The suffering and jubilation will be an exalted breath
As we return to greet what is ahead. This tremendous
Turbulent lesson of humility, this complicated uncertainty
Is the first crawl, the first step, this cry
Back to sun-flame, the wind-breath, sitting on the rock backbone
Drinking from the water's vein.
Life givers, This Great Mystery.

Harry Thurston

In Season

I. *In Another Country*

The windmills on the mountain
are at a standstill, their whirring
blades arrested.

In the deserted village,
the chattering of house sparrows,
the cooing of doves.

An empty bus passes by,
keeping its schedule, though
everyone is at home.

The roadways are empty,
miles and miles of fields
left fallow.

I imagine the animals
gone feral, wandering
without herdsmen,

the great trees,
standing alone in the wheat,
withering from drought.

And in the city,
from the open hotel window,
birdsong is heard

over the white noise
of air conditioners,
at intervals,

the din of an airplane
returning to port
for the last time.

II. *In Transit*

Now we are told to trust no one,
no surface—steel, wood, plastic,
or skin.

Masked and gloved,
we navigate the space
from here to there,

full of fear
for the common air
we breathe,

recycled in this tube,
high in the sky.
On the ground

we are pariah,
unwelcome in our own country,
immigrants to a new reality.

III. *In Quarantine*

The river, frozen
fast all winter, opens
a way over night.

In the morning
the birds arrive on cue,
as they always do.

The common mergansers christen
the waters, diving in sync,
then whirligig through the sky,

ramrod straight, their white backs
articulate, shining
with purpose.

Pairs of Canada geese swim
wing-to-wing, their voices
plaintive with longing.

In the salt ponds, black ducks
tip-up, kingfishers drop
to spear a fishy bouquet.

Our world is at rest,
theirs—so close, out there—
turns again in season.

Moni Brar

Time for Inventory

suddenly, there is time where there was none.
there is time to fill in the gaps,
to loosen the words from my tongue,
to take inventory of those I've neglected to learn.

there is time to itemize the weeds:
Prostrate
Pigweed
Shepherd's
Purse
Henbit
Dalmation
Toadflax
White
Cockle
Pale Smartweed
Hoary Cress
Flixweed

there is time to learn their Latin names:
Amaranthus
graecizans
Capsella
bursa-pastoris
Lamium .
amplexicaule
Linaria
dalmatica
Lychnis alba
Polygonum
lapathifolium
Cardaria

draba
Descurainia
Sophia

there is time to discover where they live:
drowning down a hillside
in muted green hues,
tucked in the shade circling
a ponderosa trunk,
parading through the sparse soil of
a mountain ledge,
slicing open sidewalks
and rich garden loam.

there is time to revel in how they
scent the Spring air,
feel between the toes
or in the crook of a neck,
taste on warm lips,
sway in the evening breeze
to fill the spaces
and soften all this noise.

Katherine L. Gordon

A Guilt of Covid 19

We keep washing our hands,
a MacBethian hope of outing
the damned spot of our careless creation:
Abuse of animals, pollution of planet,
greed and profit cloaking reality of poverty,
dire need, refugees despised, the poor forsaken.
We finally moved the angels to despair,
now the warning from every force in nature,
angelic admonishment:
love the planet, places of light we are privileged
to inhabit...
or lose it all in ignorance and greed.
Love of all that lives, sharing and healing,
the hard-won cure.

Bruce Meyer

Wild Turkeys

They never came close to town
let alone wandered paved streets.
But with the doors shut, traffic
silenced, and neighborhood dogs

sequestered in fenced backyards,
they reclaimed their ancestral space.
They returned because *their* plagues,
the scourges of cars and buses,

had vanished, and they survived,
finding places gleaned from legends,
wooded labyrinths where nothing
hunted them except fatted shadows –

a tom and seven hens pecking
the lawn, inviting the deer, foxes,
partridges, and birdsongs that traced
the filigree of a soundless spring

to join in their reclamation. Their meat
is bitter, and though it could feed
a famished hunter or scavengers
whose pangs rang with the wind,

they are cured now, bow their heads,
and pose as if deep in wordless prayer.
thanking the flightless spirit of ground
for returning to them what they loved.

Terry Watada

Ghost Town

dolphins
    skitter through
  Venetian canals,

wolves roam
the
con-man's footprints of
Times Square,

and birds loosen & unfurl
their wings   when
the industry clouds   lift,
carried on the arms of the wind.

i feel the golden
wheat shafts as i dream
in the
      fields of grief
in an empty town.

but

  when patches of

 blue

come together

to create a new sky,

I wonder

 if & when

   the rain

 of plague droplets

subsides to be replaced

by

 the storms

 of cynicism, enmity and

 venality;

just succumb, just…?

Carol Stephen

Ten-hut, Alligators, Ten-hut

Fear is the mask we place over our mouths
to hold in screams of desperation. Made bold by vacant streets,
alligators march in cadence, *ten-hut, sound off.* Three of them
pose as purses. The one bringing up the rear walks
backwards in time. He can smell the red viral scent
of the swamp rising in the east toward Bethlehem.

My brother says the animals are called away, there are
other places for them, ones where food lasts forever—
all of it made of plastic—wrapped for safety in the carcasses
of dead drinking straws. I don't believe it.
Il dit un mensonge, I say.

And the rear alligator moves forward in time, becomes
the forward alligator, *ten-hut.* The squadron marches west
with the virus. The air tastes salt-sweet and heavy in the day
as the ragged sun of indecision peaks at noon, begins its next descent.
You hear its sizzle and snap as it slips down the sky, nudges the river
and bounces back to heaven.

The reptiles are *gutfounded.* Each has the empty eye
of lunchtime, and we the closest sandwich. One nudges
your leg, begins to open wide. You've felt the graze of teeth,
rasp along your shinbone, seen the sheen of white pearlies
as you raise your ventilator, bring it down with a sharp crack
on the skull of the rear alligator. No respecter of rank, you.

Domestic cats are now the alligator's most feared predator.
When the hour strikes two, the cat, roused from his nap
will stretch, yawn, sharpen his feet, as cats are wont to do,
then holler "Tally-ho!" and the cat will kill himself an alligator feast.

Alligator purses, their leather tanning in the glow of setting sun.

Notes: *Il dit un mensonge*—French for *he's lying.*
gutfounded: Newfoundland dialect for hungry.

Distancing

Maureen Hynes

The First Mask

Perhaps it was a giant leaf— mullein,

say, or Sweet coltsfoot – impermanent

& doubling as a fan. Followed the mask

made of a small mammal's soft skin,

a black outline inked around the eyeholes

like the circles around a vireo's eye.

Then a strip of bark, two torn slits

for the eyes. A piece of wood,

carved, sanded, ochre-painted.

Blue feathers glued in rays

around a papier maché face. For

protection or ritual. At Samhain,

a disguise, a ruse, a jesting flirt.

Or the bandito's need to dissemble.

Now the ceremony is broadly public,

required, gauzed & elasticized.

We bare our eyes but cover the mouth

& nostrils to keep us from breathing

in a wasp or thorn, an asbestos flake,

to keep us from spray-speaking poison

in the shape of tiny beaded crowns.

Fraser Sutherland

Plague

They stride into the weather,

under bobbing umbrellas, they stride in the rain,

no matter, they also stride in the sun.

Some are pushing baby carriages

pushing as fast as the babies do.

 Out on the sidewalk, outside the house I'm in,

people are hurrying, some are running. Alone

or paired up, a man with a child, a man and woman,

Two women, two men. Across the street they do the same

except in the opposite direction.

Dogs are taking their owners for walks

with a dog trot, a jog trot.

People don't declare a destination,

they know where they go will be as bad as what they flee.

To what they flee, to what they rush toward

they give several names, some of them scientific,

one of them ending in *–emic.* Maybe endemic.

Bruce Meyer

Biography of a Pathogen

The pathogen spent decades
fleeing from our grief, had nowhere
to hide because no one loved it,
was born behind a barbed-wire fence,
shat and pissed in open streams,
and slept beside the famished.

It tried to tell us we gave it life,.
how it entered cities to stay alive,
saved enough money to buy a slum,
denied its tenants necessities of life,
turned off the water, then the heat,
and demanded to be paid in blood.

The pathogen bought an expensive car,
a big house with a swimming pool,
then a yacht, toured the world,
courted and proclaimed its leaders.
The pathogen put its brand on life,
then on bankers, and finally on us.

But nothing was ever enough for it.
It desired to know what makes us live,
or what we live for, or what we love,
said 'love is nothing and life is not less,'
then studied how we ate and slept,
and crawled inside our waking thoughts.

Now, the pathogen says we're useless,
says we're expendable: get back to work.
Says we must embrace each other,
argues we're only here for the money,
and seals its bond with a Judas kiss.
The pathogen says it's not responsible.

It is what it is. We made it huge.
It's a free country, it says of itself.
It sleeps in our minds, a dream come true.
It doesn't care if it owns us or not.
Money is more important than lives
It wants to be us and kills for the chance.

Louise B. Halfe-Sky Dancer

A Letter – wahkotowin – Relationship

I'm sorry I haven't been following the music
The music has been the broom where I've swept the debris
Mopped footsteps into the future's wait.
I've been writing
To the prairie walkers
To the sweat-lodge family
In attempt to wake up the inner peace
Where Mystery resides
Where darkness dominates like a spread sheet
Waiting for some revelation.
Yet even in sleep the virus
Finds the holes where it torments us
A storm that frightens
The semi-awake.

I haven't been ignoring you
I've been held by the hard-packed snow
As it crunches beneath my feet.
I've been entertained by coyotes
The magpies and ravens
A passing eagle. The wide grin
Of my dog.
And I've been cooking
Untried recipes, dreaming
Of the day when I can see you all.

Donna Langevin

Blue Shamrocks

March 17, 2020

We cancel the parade,
avoid ceilidths and pubs,
trade St. Patrick's regalia for
top hats with wilted blue shamrocks.
Instead of green beer,
pint glasses brim with tears.

We substitute the skirl of Uilleann bagpipes
for the drowning lung's last gurgle,
and exchange choruses
of toorahloorahloorah
for the silence of thousands
who have already died.

And yet, and yet …
Astronauts send photos
of Ireland from orbiting labs,
while we hold our somber
earthbound vigils
in private spaces.

Hugs and handshakes on hold,
our only dance is with fingers on keyboards.
Each of us now a small isle
in a global archipelago,
goodwill ships afloat
close the distance between us.

Shirley A. Serviss

The New Normal

It's the COVID game for adults. We stand in
circles chalked on the sidewalk like hopscotch.
Move one or two, sometimes three spaces ahead
as though at the roll of a die. It's not yet eight
on a Saturday morning, but we're already
lined up, bags and baskets in hand.

We drink our coffee, smell the roses along
the brick wall of the bus barn turned Famers'
Market, study the murals, listen to the musician
across the street sing *Hallelujah* as we wend
our slow way to the finish line—no snakes
to slide down, no ladders to climb. No "Mother,
may I?" as security lets us through the door.

"No social lingering" warned the sign outside,
but how can we not stop to talk to vendors
we've known for years: Catfish Coffee, Grandma
Bear's, where we buy our bread. Recognized
and called by name, despite our disguises.
True in-person visits too rare these months
of Google Hangouts, FaceTime and Zoom.

Rhona McAdam

Home is a Different Country

Now I am back
And home is a different country
- John Burnside

The house has never been cleaner
the streets quieter
the buses more empty
churning the night, every light on,
every seat free
but one.

Life has got
so small. There is no front
to report from.
Everywhere you look you
don't see it.
No one yet knows
what it looks like
so it's hard to hide from.

Still, we take shelter
and measures against it.
Our hands have never been cleaner
our larders more curiously stocked
our agendas more empty.

TV lights flicker
in the neighbours' curtains
as if they had company
into the small hours.
The news, the news, the news.

I stay home, a new cliché.
Sewing masks.
Baking bread.

Wither now
the woman from the pool
with the evil eye.
The ill-tempered waitress
from the coffee shop.
The bastard who left me.

A cold bright spring
pours its heart out.
The mountains
have never been clearer.

On walks the strangers pass
averting faces as if
a glance might smite them.

Out shopping
we play sluggish games of hopscotch
on the floor's markings.
Everything takes longer.

Trying not to breathe
we mumble in our masks,
gesture with our raw clean hands.

Wolves and cougars
take a few liberties
in our empty streets.

The sun in children's paintings
has always been
the colour of the tape
now enfolding our playgrounds.

Erin Moure

How to write poetry

There was nothing different
or it was the same

I had grief at a window
meaning
we had grief, there was no window

Grief was something we "had"?
We ached the long way round
Little fists of bright leaves emerged
        up and down the straights
        of branches

It was spring, an infection
ran amok in persons known
not known

Persons on the street vanished
and returned
between equinox and solstice
Droves like us, we said
Droves like us

and a woman on a third-floor balcony in the wind,

holding up a blue watering can.

(the garbage truck goes by,

a garbage man coughing)

Debbie Ulrich*

WHAT I SEE

We as a world are in this together.

Stand!

Heads kept high underneath the masks.

Finding the light that brings us together as a whole.

Help each other survive in this darkest of time.

We wait.

No celebrations yet.

See only through locked windows.

Happy for Face-time and Skype.

See the outside world and faces through glass.

Talk to family and friends, new people too.

Everywhere.

To finally connect.

Close and far away.

*Debbie Ulrich is a resident in a long term care facility, Camrose. In an instant, this middle aged working mother needed to create a new, meaningful and happy life as a quadriplegic due to a freakish car accident in 2002. She has overcome many limitations in beauty. She first relearned to do vital tasks that we do almost inherently at birth: swallowing, drinking, coughing, and bending an arm. Establishing and re-establishing nerve pathways with a mountain range of determination, pain, anguish and support from family and friends. Regaining some independence opened opportunities for her to learn some firsts: rolling a wheelchair, driving a power wheelchair (a driver test needed to be passed), painting and using a computer (which also required relearning how to spell words like 'cat').

The arts have been therapeutic for her. Painting enables her to incorporate colour from her art work into her daily life, which changes every day. The experience of writing the story of her accident and the long road to recovery has helped her to express herself more coherently and realize that despite her limitations she is still a whole person. Her story (assisted by Janet Enns), *Somewhere over the Rainbow* is published n the anthology *Beauty Everyday: Stories from Life as it Happens (2016)*. She has appeared on CBC's Radio Active program and in a TELUS film about community. Her latest creative expression is this poem.

Anna Mioduchowska

Virus Trap

o
o n
o n i
o n io
onionio
oni o nio
oni o nio
oni o nio
oni o nio
oni o nio
oni o nio
onio nio
onio
non
ion
onio
nonion
oninonioniononionio
onionionionionionioniono
onionionionionionionionionionio
onionionionionionionionionnionnio
onionionionioninionionionionionioio
onionionionionionCOVID-19onionionionio
onionionionionionionionionionionionio
onionionionionionionionionionionionio
onionionionionionionionionionio
onionionionionionio
onion

44

Fear and Quarantine

Donna Friesen

Covid Sounds

If we had put our ears to earth
Perhaps we would have heard it.

The overture that opened slow,
And low,
Inaudible to us,
Drowned out
By pounding waves on beaches
Of our Springbreak vacations.

Those first discordant notes
Plucked randomly on strings
Of Chinese violins;
How those first notes
Became a theme
Repeated, exponentially
In global variations.
Some modern composition
Growing ever louder
More insistent
Never quite achieving resolution
A keening for the dead
Who never heard their named good-byes.

The world's antiphonal response
The wail of sirens slicing through
The thickness of our grief,
The slitting open of the scant few
Treasure troves of PPE,
The grind of motors, fabricating masks.
All insufficient counterpoint
To allegretto viral spread.

The thrumming bass that underlies it all a dirge of isolation silence.
Scant childrens' laughter in our streets, the office banter stilled.
Our concert halls and theatres
A single, solemn chord of emptiness.
The only constant—
Swish of doors in sterile wards
Foreclosing contact with the sick.

But if we put our ears to earth
Perhaps there's something different that we'll hear.

The spouting of our whales
No longer stressed by noise.
The hooves of goats that clatter on cement returned to claim their home
In empty streets in Wales.
And here, where Spring returns
A welling up of birdsong
In jet free
Blue sky
Symphonies.

Thomas Trofimuk

The cranes

The nurse who tested us (because we returned north from the US at the start of a pandemic) was suited up with a mask and a face shield, scrubs, and gloves. Waiting our turn, we sat in a waiting room with a few dozen other masked people – wondered if there was someone in the room who actually was sick. We willed ourselves not to scratch any itch – not to touch our faces, and certainly, even if there was a tickle, NOT to cough. Smiling behind our masks, our eyes became our only vulnerability – the only way in. We were a little frightened and our nurse calmed us. *It's painless*, she said. *And if you're not showing symptoms, you're likely fine.* She took away our anxiety and I wondered what she did with it. Did she carry it? Or did it fall to the floor to be swept away? The test was uncomfortable for a moment, and then, we were off into the world of isolation, physical distancing, and so many unknowns, to wait for the results.

Weeks beyond, on a warm-sun, cool-breeze afternoon, there are Sandhill Cranes, hundreds of them, flying north, overhead. Flying in a series of loosey-goosey Vs, they sound like a thousand pigeons cooing. I look up from my yard work and am humbled. How is it I deserve to see and hear these cranes? It is easy to imagine a kinship – me in my backyard, cleaning the leaves in the corners under the linden and the poplars along the fence – doing what is needed. And the cranes, cooing north in their ridiculous Vs because that journey is needed. Of course, it's not the same. I am no Sandhill Crane. We humans choose to clean our yards – while cranes are driven by something instinctual, wild, raw. Soon, I will stop for a small glass of whisky and perhaps a cigar. The cranes, I suspect, will keep flying north. I watch as they disappear beyond my neighbours' rooftops – and can hear them long after they're gone. They vanish into blue sky. They are swallowed into cerulean blue.

Then, I remember the nurse. I remember her eyes were blue – they were kind, and tired, and blue.

Tania Carter

Covid

Where the fear is based in entitlement
Those beneath are unworthy
Of compassion and empathy

Where the fear is based in entitlement
The scripts of others
Remain unheard and unrealized

There are people out there
Who believe they are entitled
To feel better than others
based on the virtue of entitlement
They went to school for more years
Their family spends more money
Their family is richer than others
They exploited the world with more fervour
Without thought or compassion

The world is in demise, based on the news
The world is covered in a silk cloth and blood
Stained the world needs to come back to its own
Outside of fear and reflect on what it is and wants
To be

We are the world, on a minute scale
We start from there
the person holding the pen
Or typing the keys and write our story
With our own fears, our own strategies of how to be
How to get beyond the fear
To move to a better place

Fear is an emotion like happiness
We were happy four months ago
Now we are not, the world is not

We are but one individual
One drop in the cosmos
We can be happy with a change of mind

Like a movie can interrupt our emotions
Veer us this way or that

We are more than a swinging pendulum
Or a feather in the wind
We can make up our minds
To be happy
Not to fear so much
Not to feed this fear

We have the strength and capacity
Sometimes we can do it alone
Sometimes we need others
....many times
And that's okay

We are segregated
Government calls it isolated
Government calls it voluntary
We can be of one mind – still
We can still be united
We can still build strength in each other
We can still be
Ourselves
Whole and unfearful.

Kate Marshall Flaherty

Bridge Pose

Mid-March 2020

What am I bridging, I ask the water.
I'm strong and flexible, but at times,
in the middle of my arch, I fear
the weight will buckle,
my flexion will fall
into rapids.

I imagine a *bridge over troubled water*,
the Billy Goat Gruff's suspension,
golden gate overpass;
each rises and lifts over something
dangerous—

Is that it? We rise and *trip-trap* over
fear itself? We close our eyes and run.

My heels dig into mat, shoulders
spread to ground, wing-blades widening—

an ache in my heart tickles, sharp
as beard bristles; I have been a goat, too gruff
in the face of corona virus, too sure-footed and
silly, convinced it was over there on the other side.

I breathe in bridge pose, imagining
            as I trip-trap, blindfolded,
                    over troll's rickety span, hoping
            to cross raging waters just
one foot at a time.

Heidi Greco

Moral dilemma

As I walked past the oldest house on my street, a place I'd always been curious about, the front door began to open. A man, extremely thin and pale, stepped out into the sunlight, ducking as he passed beneath the lintel. When I greeted him, he blurted that his wife was dead, lying inside the house, and approached me, his skinny arms extended longingly, seeking the comfort of a hug. I could see that he'd been crying and knew that my rejecting him would only make him feel worse. But these were still the days of standing-apartness, and who could know what his woman had died of.

Carley Mayson

We Forget Her Shape

*Response to Cobra Collins' poems on COVID-19

I'll toss some hand sanitizer off the balcony
to you, raise it like a lantern, while the red, white, blue
lights bounce by
in a sky we don't recognize anymore
I'll sketch you the last emergency
I put my hands on, palms crushing
a chest, Naloxone pushed in, witnessed death reversed
a gaping mouth inhaling fresh
oxygen, same way, I gulp on hope
that stars start to notice us in all our muted,
minuteness   my feet still on the concrete of the balcony
you down on my front lawn, toes in grass coated
in COVID. My neighbour is mummified
in stolen hospital masks
and hoarded toilet paper, suffocated by her own
 shields by now the sanitizer should have dropped on the lawn,
missing
your hands   the lights   are gone. We echo "is this the
apocalypse
 yet?"
does the big dipper know we forget
her shape? I light
optimism and inhale. She does, she knows you
and me in this dark
"is this the apocalypse yet?"

Jocko Benoit

Searching For Mario

I spend a whole day searching
for Mario and his console,
but more people understand
in this self-quarantine how
video games fill the hole
futility keeps mining and stores
are sold out, no matter how many
leads my wife tracks down online.
She is an adept of shopology –
that proposes every need can be met
with the right product and that new
products arrive exactly when a need
is born. Buy when the buying is good.

Now she needs the right elastics
and the right material for masks
because sloppy hygiene is not
an acceptable aesthetic and I keep
using too many sanitizing wipes
per trip. She is beginning to regret+
her choice of mate, albeit from
a limited market – maybe next time
a mustachioed plumber looking
for his princess, turning in a maze
of coins and powers and with
a couple of lives to spare.

Brian Day

Unskinned

These are the days when no one goes swimming,
the pool unbroken, pristine, alluring,
and touch is exiled to a foreign country.

We bump against the imagined breath of neighbours,
carry with us a new weight of space:
physically, chemically, neutral, inert.

We enter a fiction of expendable bodies,
encased in these exoskeletons of caution,
haunted by the memory of our tactile lives.

My flesh thirsts each time I pass the pool,
remembering generous water on my skin,
the brightness of a body sheathed in wet.

These are the days when the ocean is closed,
beaches and shorelines forbidden to our feet,
a walk in the forest transgressive, illicit.

We inhabit a world where dancing is outlawed,
showers and gyms are locked against us,
and hugs take place in vacant air.

These are the days when caress is violation,
hand on skin a cause for rebuke,
any intimacy condemned as criminal.

We know our bodies are made for embrace,
for each cool immersion in animating water,
each enlivening frisson of skin on skin;

to be meetings of breath and liquid and lip,
to be creatures keen with exultation of touch,
from nuzzle to the full concertos of nakedness.

Our bodies have been excised from our lives.
We are the breaking of all that precedes us,
abducted from every sleek animal we are.

Laura Swart

We're All in This Together

1.
i'm ashamed
she said
ashamed to be Chinese
my grandmother slaughtered chickens in the backyard
turtles and rabbits, too
our neighbors despised us
picked up stones to stone us
but Jesus?
he bent over
and wrote their names in the dust.

2.
Outbreak! Outbreak at Canada Post!
I scroll down hungrily.
Has it taken us, finally?
Are we defeated?
What is the number?
How many dead?
1000? 100?
Five.
Sick, not dead.
But enough.
Enough to inflate the ubiquitous voices.
And Florence, a refugee,
For one more day
Leaves her children with their abusive father
While she works on the frontline
The daycare doors sealed shut with a heart.

3.
My shopping cart unwittingly slips over the six-foot line
And a woman shields her face with her arms, shouting,
Get back! Get back!
I steer away
Try to move my cart up another aisle
But the wheels won't turn
They want to go straight
And ram right into her
Then a priest reaches out, steadies my cart, and falls down dead.

4.
I have a dark spot on my left cheek
It's spreading
And I can't find a doctor
So I go out on my balcony and join the others
Who are banging big pots with soup spoons, serving spoons, wooden
spoons
Gongs and drums, banners and flags.

The noise reaches to Heaven and settles into the prayer bowls there
We bang for exactly five minutes
To honor the front-liners when their shift changes
And new doctors and new nurses arrive to guard the hallowed halls
Of the vacant hospital.

My spot grows larger, even overnight
But for five minutes we come together and make a joyful noise
And the noise binds us together
Like an egg yolk and its attendant white
Just before you separate them, beat the whites,
And toss the yoke down the drain.

5.
Long line to get in
But I'm a Corrections Officer
The prisoners, most of them, have been released—
All but the murderers and rapists
Assaults and break-ins are up by 150 percent
But that's okay
Someone has to be the sacrificial lamb.
I bypass the lineup
And they all step aside, let me pass
I do my grocery shopping
Unmolested
Then go to the prison
And wipe excrement off an inmate
Who has shit herself.

6.
We constructed a zipline in the backyard for the kids
they climb into the bucket, fasten thr straps
and ride
suspended between present and the future
but the parents bottom out halfway;
they are heavy with fear.

7.
He passes fettuccine al pesto to me
through an open window
his face is veiled
like Adam's was
before the first animal was slaughtered
and so much was lost.
Then he turns
lowers his mask
lifts the Cup to his lips
and takes a long drink.

8.
Yesterday I found a half-nest dangling in my lilac tree,
A cup, a dip of mud
Pressed into a little arc
I held it in my hands, this shallow dip
And wondered where the owners were.
Did they try again
After their home and work were taken?
I placed the nest gently on my gate
To remind me that gateways still exist.

Tanja Bartel

I am the Lonely Part of My Day

Speaking to an audience of air and one chair from my pulpit,
I adore the bone structure of my hands

when I watch them unfold and describe my hours.
A waste of elegant curving gestures.

I've shredded the day into separate strips: eat, pace, window-watch.
Gargling loud as I please in silk pajamas.

I'm a portrait above the sink and again in the hall.

No man is an island, but a woman is a penthouse.
I am my homeland with stations set up

according to the limits of the floor plan.
A piecemeal setup. Here a sleeping area, there a dish pit.

Each emotion, too, shelters in its place—a patchwork
of wailing, next to painting, next to terror, beside curiosity.

A beetle on its back has no friends to flip it back to life side.

Night, the dénouement of the final episode,
where I dream my doctor, who becomes

my daughter is driving a convertible
and I'm in the passenger seat. She's speeding

through a construction zone and there's a giant
hole in the asphalt we go through and down.

I have just enough time to put both arms around her,
say, *I love you honey*, and we crash

soft as laundry tossed on a bed.
The bone structure of our greatest fear

is actually boneless, soft.
And we hear neither clamour nor crash.

Christine Smart

Reaching Out

Pink camellia blossoms flow along
Morningside road to the harbour
by the miniature post office, flanked
by the ferry dock and Rocksalt café—
they flow the way foot passengers
and ferry traffic bustles and rolls.

In March, when I last wrote you,
the postmistress sold me a stamp,
passed over change for a fiver,
said: *this village is turning
into a ghost town.* Between ferries
dead quiet: three people separated by six
feet on the street: one cultivates dread locks,
one disguised under an orange toque,
another plays flute.

This week the car deck, half-vacant,
few cars and trucks pour off the ramp,
trundle uphill home to isolate.
Roads deserted, shops barred.
Shift change on the dock, fluorescent-
vested deckhands scurry,
an empty public bus waits.

The post office sign: CLOSED.
No stamp for my envelope. I trace
your name, longhand script in black ink.
I promised you a letter day.
The camellia blossoms
wither on the street.

Giovanna Riccio

Home-sick

A story out of a bat cave,
set in invisible ink afflicts the headlines
a cimmerian microbe blights garden and street
flings spring into lockdown—

given the opacity of tomorrow, of airports in a chokehold,
our wings collapse—stranded,
dragging sagging hearts, we head indoors.

Flashing a punk-spiked crown, this viral marauder
wields exponential power, dictates bulletins,
updates the death count, outlaws touch
as it proliferates via lips and hands.
Statisticians and medics crunch numbers, ride
vectors and peaks, map deadly intersections
where each neighbour or passerby veils the odds.

Where each citizen disfigures the social contract,
two metres mandate mortal isolates;
with wary looks, we damn each other,
shun hugs, shed the pat on the back.
Under a sky gasping for oxygen, corpses pile up,
eyeing hazmat-suited nurses mirroring hellish
sisters-of-mercy—we settle for air kisses.

Borders toughen and turn icy, bristle with searchlights,
each beam pins stranger to strangling invader.

At breakneck speed the mace-like butcher
lacerates the poor, penetrates slaughterhouses
and prison cells, slashes elders damned
to infernal retirement *havens* where bankers
hurl barbed stars at the homesick perdu.

And aren't we all legislated homebodies now— homesick for air?
Sizing up our clannish cages, we pace
between grandma's handwritten recipes and legible screens,
blow out virtual birthday candles and make a wish
for *this* to end. Grounded in domesticity, long days
echo the tempo of sourdough and seedlings.

Exiled from this long-suffering earth, we circle
in bubbles, turn inward and unclock,
kid around and lose at Payday—poignant
the housebound eros of familiar hands
and afternoon smooching.

Our brides, proms and feasting are snuffed,
theatres and eateries barred until further notice,
with work and play bound in yellow caution-tape,
life's bustling whirl screeches to a dead stop—

deserted streets throw up the homeless,
benched, with no roof to shelter-in-place; each day
bares the rawboned body of caregivers and migrant workers,
bilked as they scrub toilets and fill the fridge,
a wing and a prayer, their only PPE.

Two metres is not the social distance separating us,
it's the rift between homeless and housed,
the gulf between essential and non-essential,
the chasm between have and have-not,
exposed and cleft deeper by an equalizing virus
unmasking the fault plaguing us.

Shelley A. Leedahl

The Quiet

So pronounced it takes a shape. It desires
the syllables of a name.

On Saturday night streets,
in this white-walled townhouse

punctuated by a red couch
like a garish smear of lipstick

against the north wall:
silence.

This non-sound the definition of time
invisibly rolling forward

against future shores.
Yes, the creek still sings

it's silver song, and at 7:00 pm
neighbours ritualistically ring bells

and the firehall siren clears the air
with its salute to healthcare workers,

but then its back to the inflamed quiet.
Perhaps a check-in with the news,

though now every other tragedy
is made so much worse

because of the collective backdrop.
It's getting dangerous to breathe.

Don't get me wrong: I'm not unhappy,
but I have become superstitious,

not tempting fate with even a thought
toward the moment a vaccine might blossom.

And I'm cautious, going back to the old ways:
hiding rolls of money in the house,

towering canned food
in the basement

beside the camping gear
I am not using.

Surreptitiously preparing, in case of anarchy,
a bloodbath—

　　　　　　I should not have said that.
I must be a quiet house

in this mute and quivering sci-fi movie
we're all trying to reach the end of.

The soundtrack is silence
and it's disconcerting, foreign—

like casualty numbers in Africa,
like mysteries we may never pronounce.

Isolation

George Elliott Clarke

Manifesto of the New Untouchables

I.

Now that we shall not touch—
now that we are all Untouchables
(unless we mask our kissless mouths,
or enact Magritte's veiled faces bussing),

we must learn to waltz solo with wind,
or hug only in fossilized, family photos,
or float aerosolized kisses, as calibrated
and as fairy-dusted as fraud artists'

investment portfolios.
Our foes? We only flog their ghosts!
Anyway, *Enmity* fritters away
as we strike and strike at wisps;

for, what good do we do to be riled up
by phantoms, impervious to scratches
or wounds of actual attack—
given our lock-down—

our "self-isolation" (with the jobless, but lustful)?
Sugary hallelujahs once accorded
diplomas, trophies, or nice pay packets,
now resonate in freshly vigorous beds....

(Solitary interests soon lose interest.)
The private brooding—*Dismissiveness*—
in each dead-end haven
quick succeeds to a noisy priority:

The coltish wildness of thighs pivoting,
riveting upon each other,
to forge the screened, preening fetus.
Meanwhile, some lovers ramble

in butterfly mode—flitting,
fluttering, alighting here and there—
flirting, if not touching.
Beautiful are their tentative desertions!

Bountiful are their emotive exertions
at escape, the heart right fitful—
no matter where we bunk, hunker
down, separate in detached union

in the in many ways absolutely
intangible failure of fellow *Feeling*....
Isn't each citizen a huddled creature
to comfort and cuddle?

In the obstinate disintegration
of neighbourhood *Charity*,
we become individualistic shoppers—
euphoric charlatans—

reveling in beatitudes—vicissitudes—
of *Loneliness*, of our solitary cells.
But I prefer to perish in an atmosphere
of petals, if I can't be as immune

as is the ultra-socially-distant sun.
At the end, dance my coffin
upon grave, suave, strong men's shoulders
before I'm merrily buried

(a brain and spine ending in an anus;
one more abandoned leaf, castaway)
in that No-Man's-Land of skeletal
remains, of reverence for ambulances,

where slide—skid—our dead—pitiful—
as the unresolved crashes of kites.

II.

2020?
This preposterous *Annus Horribilis*—
Year of the Rat
and bullish alarms,

we are thralls of an obese virus—
fatty, oleaginous—
itself a stealthy, serial killer
(not like bronchitis and crap like that).

But our death throes do not trigger *its*!
And scholarship itself is useless
to thwart the covert disease—
its malicious corruption of every touch….

Come, register its mastery of trifles—
so the most innocent noun is plagued,
or we become spiteful truants
in our fugitive abodes, taught to shun other

citizens, listlessly drifting in dawn's
suddenly disagreeable light,
unable to nuzzle into each other's breath
or to beautify whatever's gone dull.

As irritable as unscabbed sores,
we're left to nibble on dribbling tears—
to swallow vomit, the heritage of *Grief,*
for it's useless to snarl at corpses....

And it's cheerless too. We sulk and
we grumble, for we discover
there's no gratification of weeping.
We suffer wounds that do not suffer

doctoring; for we can't be touched!
We're untouched save by the sticky germ—
it's invisible, but insane *Antagonism.*
We strive to breathe but barely dare to live.

So now generic gangrene rots the heart!
Our faces—mask-banished, or mask-truncated,
are obliterated by our beloveds' erasing tears—
their sobs—defacing our obituaries!

Barb Thomas

Fractals

These days
a slice of myself
works   over   time
navigating digital forests of warnings
trudging neighbourhood silences
distress-waving my 90-year-old neighbour
crouching numb   in the ever-lengthening
projections   to a new normal

another fragment
cooks   cleans   runs a meeting
watches an ant climb the winter-caked window

a portion
rises with the light
writing together the night shards
grasping their symmetry   how each is a whole
sliver of social brokenness
fractal of covid-19
the virus   a fractal of us

our dreams are fractals too
reflecting our light   taking our shape
holding our children
feeding community
making our way   by moonlight

Amanda Perry

Week Three

"I can still take the sun,"
he says, relief as his accent,
and of course he means tomar el sol,
but the accidental grandiosity he gives
to a garden, private enough to not
be abolished
catches in my ear and throat.

It's week three of enclosure so
I'm calling my exes.

They're contained by congealed
borders, the compression that
rules out those infra-tricks which
were structures, the highways and
slipstreams that made hours
out of space. Nearness is less
numerical now.

Their answers are forms of the same:

The tallies, the measures, the guess
that is hope or faith or hints of mutiny.
The last of them reads cheap sci-fi
in a Tel Aviv basement and battles
with proofs; the first in Dubai
considers if expatriation
may expire.

Here in my split-tongued city
I suck in each
voice like an event.
Montréal's half-aborted
spring is still coming.
I accept the matte clumping
on trees as flowers.

Nothing happens, really.

No knots are sliced or tied
but when all contact is anyway illicit
why not swallow up the shadow
of old touches
these unsanitized hands
that wave from a distance
and reach to take the sun.

Glen Sorestad

Afternoon Chat

After two months of social distancing,
self-isolating, and living our lives
as if we were the last two humans left,

we visit with our long-time friends
who have also bungalowed themselves
in their own quarantine thoughts.

We meet in their backward for
BYOB glasses of wine, our two-metre
wines, as we call them; it seems

almost as if there is initial fumbling
for what we should say -- a hesitance
to begin, where do we start?

as if perhaps we need to re-learn
the natural agenda-less chat:
what do we always talk about?

In the past two months of social
isolation, it seems our language
skills and usual glib small talk,

our quick apt repartees have fled,
deserted us, become lost in a chasm
of discarded and forgotten words.

Glen Sorestad

Walking with the Coronavirus

So here we are, walking a neighbourhood
sidewalk daubed with the grubby detritus
of disappearing winter, keeping a watchful

eye out for other walkers who might not be
inclined to distance themselves the mandated
two metres social distance, feeling a bit

elated just to breathe fresh air rather than
the well lived-in housebound mélange
of aromas, odors, and that indefinable

lived-in smell two people impart to a home
over twenty years of occupancy, pleased
to be outside after the early telltale signs

of encroaching cabin fever burrowing under
the skin of comfort, quicker and more insidious
than the coronavirus itself. We meet

wave after wave of fellow walkers, singles
and couples, families taking advantage
of a robin's egg blue sky, muscling March sun

doing its best to purge the air of pestilence
in a single afternoon. We call out hellos to all,
like the island castaways, returned home;

our fellow walkers sing out their responses,
though all are strangers, but for the moment
we are bonded each to each in need and desire

to be at one with the sudden beauty of Spring,
as if the day was just a temporary thing,
as if the viral pandemic was fake news.

Chris Bullock

What We Choose

"Good choice," says my co-facilitator, when
I agree to cancel the poetry and song circle.
"Good choice," says my guitar teacher,
when I agree to cancelling the group lesson.
Exactly what choice did I have, I ask, silently.
Yes, I could choose to discuss poems
in an empty room, play my pieces
while the teacher shouts advice from the kitchen.
I feel my fear of abandonment fueling
a fierce protest against get-togethers
cancelled, travel plans in tatters,
empty shelves and closed borders.

I walk to the one event left, St. Patrick's
Day outdoors, bring your own Guinness,
meet next to the statue of an Irish pioneer.
No-one is there, nothing next to the statue
except a profusion of Christmas roses.
I stand there looking at them, suddenly still.
Their presence takes my breath away.
Then I remember the young man outside
the store saying we were the first people
he'd seen not carrying endless rolls of toilet paper,

talking about his shopping for the elderly.
I remember passing, on the way here,
a man on a park bench with a Martin guitar.
He's playing a Bach partita immaculately
while a split seam in his jacket leaks cotton.
He says he regularly plays for the homeless
in the park, until, always about this time,
they get too rowdy and he retreats
to this bench to play for himself.

I walk back through the quiet streets.
The sky seems clearer than when I came,
like the clear blue sky the residents of Wuhan
are apparently seeing for the first time.
I didn't choose that an event I wanted
to take place didn't, that a young man
touched my heart with his kindness,
that I would get to hear guitar music,
that I would see flowers and not crowds.
I didn't choose any of this whole cascade
of cancellations and surprises, and yet,
walking with my unused cans of Guinness
clanking in my backpack, I seem to be
--for a moment perhaps, or perhaps for a life—
walking towards a world which I sense
I would choose with all my heart.

Josephine LoRe

Waiting

April 29, 2020

> Words waited for, sometimes days, weeks
>   materialize while hands fold a towel
>
> — *Joan Shillington*

Words waited for, sometimes days, weeks
materialize while hands fold a towel
Stir a soup of broccoli and jasmine rice, sharp cheddar
While I walk under silver dusk sky
Notice the first tree burst into unnamed spring

Words come for the crows, three in a tree
For the mallards, drake and hen in the pond
For the waxwing, rowanberries in beak
For the hares who chase lightheartedly in deserted roadway
For the poke of tulip, ruddy brown, bravely four inches high

For the bags of leaves swept out of beds
For the chives and rhubarb who survived winter
For the pansies yet to shine their faces of violet and yellow
For the iris yet to blade into the sky in majestic amethyst
For the French lilac I pruned in the hopes of more abundant bloom

Words come for faces on the screen
From across this continent and across the sea
For whom my empty arms ache and ache
For words that reach my soul and take lodging
From my students who struggle in this time of upside-down

We read of the Black Death in school
Ring around the Rosie, Pocket full of Posie
Convinced epidemic was something of the past
Something that happened somewhere else, long ago

I sent a gift to a poet friend
A poem unfinished, asking for his flourish
Thinking how sweet the collaboration would be
And he sent me back
thanks
and thanks
And told me words would not come
His head trapped in a plastic bag
He suffocates in covid
His wings clipped

And I thought of the Waterboys
Whose wings have been clipped
Whose shoes have been stuck with glue
And I want to share their wisdom with my friend
That he too may take this broken wing and learn to fly

But we are cocooned in our own pain
Our own isolating loss
Our own unfloatable bubble of heaviness

A girl in my class who was more porcupine than pussycat
Who'd learned to distrust grown-ups with their painted smiles and
brittle hearts
Sent me a photo series today of herself and her grandpa
Building a mini picnic table for Bernard,
    the squirrel that lives in her tree
And there he is, Bernard taking peanuts from a cup
On a table built by four loving hands, two beaming hearts

It is what allows us to survive, this capacity to love
Beyond all other needs
The simple need to love and be loved

And so I send sweet doves out
                    into the gloaming sky

Colin Morton

Tripping the Rideau Canal (TVO)

Sated, numbed, I am becoming part of the furniture,
part of the couch I am crouched on for safety.
The flat screen surrounds me with green, unfurls
before me the river at a walking pace,
past woods and fields, early autumn maples
reddening, weeping willows overshadowing
docks in the yards of riverfront houses.
Birds glide past the bow-mounted camera
as a small craft slides into Long Island locks
and, when the lock master cranks opens the gate,
rides down a single step toward the Capital.
Ducks on the surface, undisturbed, part for the boat,
gulls overhead go on with their conversations.
An hour passes, two hours, I am become furniture,
the boat glides unhurried through its green domain.
Up ahead, I know, is Hog's Back Falls,
more locks at Carleton, then Dow's Lake,
the long urban stretch of canal toward the Chateau.
But slow down. The day is fine, sun bright, river calm.
I am safe inside where the virus can't reach me,
there's no rush and nowhere I'm needed, only
the sun on the Rideau and this day to survive.

Ian FitzGerald

Decibels

Steel wheels on pavement,
unmistakably skateboard, rolling through an empty parkade.
Intermittent silences signal jumps ...

then landings,

Voices echo, amid the COVID calm,
amplified this late-melting April
by the absence of other sounds.

3 p.m. on a Thursday.

Fewer horns
Fewer bells
Hammering on hold
Engines all on pause.

Skaters skate and
in this longing quiet,
our decibels are taking
their time.

George Melnyk

I Wonder

I wonder what you see
of this
    that I cannot see
    what surrounds the
    opaque present
    of illness, pain, death
    all aggregated in a grand
    numbers game
    that explains
    abstractly each feeling,
    thought and mood.

Can we worry together,
the living and the living
hold hands across
the chasms of our separation
walled in, walled out
forever hoping for an end
to begin all over again?

Carol Casey

Pandemic Grand-parenting

How will it be when
I tell you not to climb
on my knee for hugs and kisses,
not to stick your fingers
in my mouth and nose,
not hold you tight,
our bodies melting
into each-other?

What will you think
with your half-formed
primal vocabulary?
Will it break your heart
as it does mine,
but without the safety net
of comprehension?

Will you think it's you,
that touch is wrong,
that closeness can't be trusted
that people turn away,
that shelters often falter?
That's a lot to know at two,
to have take form
to grow a core around.

Will it mark you,
turn to monster in your happy
night-time garden?
Will you ever know
how much I want it different
how much I want
my touch to say to you?

Betsy Struthers

Distance Learning

We are in our separate rooms, doors closed, listening
to the dark. No one is rifling through the kitchen drawers,
no one is creaking up the stairs, no need for our hearts to be racing,
to hold our breath. Sirens echo in the streets,
where no one waits at the crosswalk for the go.

We are in our house, drifting from window to window. Could
mop the floors, scrub the shower grout white. Next door's toddler
howls, bangs on their living room panes. His mother texts
excuses for his noise. He's stopped trying to talk, has forgotten
what adults conversing in person sound like. We understand,
tapping our keyboards, sending coded words to one another.

We are in the backyard, tramping circles in the grass. How we miss
the handshake, the hug, the air kiss cheek to cheek. We will each
take the dog on our allotted walk around the block, reel in her leash
when a neighbour approaches, backing off six feet. We might nod,
turn our heads away, elbow tightly clamped on buttoned lips.

We are in a meeting with our friends in boxes on the screen, wait
our turn to tell what's new. There's nothing new but news. Some of us
can't read books any more, some fed up with Netflix. All this time
for solitaire. One shows the seven masks his daughter made for him.
He likes the plain blue, finds the puppy print foolish, the flag a bit
too much, and the skull and crossbones he can't bear to touch.

Alex Manley

Lost Spring

They're saying nature is healing and offer proof: The x are
returning to the y in Venice, adjective nouns climb Welsh
garden walls. In Montreal, little has changed: the wildlife ruling
the city's still the unrepentant party animals. Your neighbours'
steady stream of guests baying clear through the *papier maché*
walls. But over time, I know, everything trends towards
nothingness. Time & again I wake, then after a time, return to
unearned sleep. From deep within the fortress of my solitude—
I'm kidding, of course. I'm only on the couch in the living
room, watching through the screen of my laptop as the
extroverts struggle with the weight of it all. Mourners of a lost
spring, etc. For them, each budding leaf a sort of new death. I
get it. To me, the lives of others always felt like a far-off insult.
Each & every piece of laughter peeled off the citrus of their
happiness. A stinging thing. A lonely eye. At least now the
playing field's been levelled. Oh, but. I really should check my
privilege. It's just. I'm so *used* to this. Spending weeks at a time
under the glow of a sadness lamp & a slow-growing sheen of
dried sweat. Watching the forest green Nature Valley wrappers
accrete, crumpled-up kleenexes multiply, apple cores appearing
here & there, slow-browning in entropy. Days like this, I feel
like I understand that one town in Ontario: Penetanguishene. I,

too, have an over-the-top sorrow close to the centre of me. Let
me tell you how this goes: Nothing happens. And after that,
more nothing. That's only the nature of things. But you knew
that already, didn't you? What *I* want to know is, when all of
this is over, will things go back to normal? Or will someone
have developed a vaccine for all the loneliness in my veins?
Will you have found a place for me somewhere in the grand arc
of your life, the way I've been keeping a place for you in mine?
It's just the inequality I mind, I swear. Will we recognize the
right moment spontaneously, the way movie characters know
when to kiss each other? Will we ourselves still
be recognizable? Crawling from our separate
platonic caves, aburst with body &
desire, weak from the cudgels
of our selves, the way the
sea uses each grain of
sand to wear the
other grains
down to no
thing?

Brian Bartlett

From *Spring 2020*

Behind the windows
of bus after bus, one
stranger, or two

In a desk, in a dark
classroom, mould eats
a forgotten orange

My watch is broken,
watch shops shut-down—
but time's loosened

A bored tattoo-artist
rests on his front steps,
empty hands upturned

Frayed, faded posters:
concerts, plays, dances,
nothing new announced

Pandemic profits—
thriving on-line market in
Escher-patterned masks

A laid-off bouncer
keeps busy—throws cement chunks
at a brick wall

In a skateboard park
the joy of recklessness
awaits resurrection

A girl whose grandma
made a Monarchy scrapbook
keeps a Covid file

One gulf narrowed—
books home-delivered
by a knapsacked cyclist

Missing the thrill of
strangers, a child waves wildly
at the garbageman

Even in sick times,
HOUSE FOR SALE soon
replaced by HOUSE SOLD

She counts her apple tree's
blossoms, then her days
of isolation

Virus be damned—
one dog-walker can't resist
another walker's dog

On today's walk
the beauties of wind-chimes
outnumber human voices

A parking lot stagnates
where many met weekly
for Cosmic Bingo

Grief

Sarah Xerar Murphy

85 Days

A Covid chronology

... containing numbers and some thoughts mixed up this June 9th about what it is to be sitting in the same position 85 days since I last touched another human being of all things hugging an acquaintance at a reading in Maine one day before lockdown when I found myself after getting home going over the opening of my new novel of the plagues that upon European contact took out at a minimum 85% of the population of the Americas a book which began in an incident 24 years ago to give me its first line 12 years later: Thus it is said that in a time long before SARS...

...only to have that simple line become by the time I start to work on the book again 9 years after that: Thus it is said that in a time long before the microcephalics of Zika or even SARS though in the time of Ebola if not of its epidemics the fastest of the slower killing times of HIV by then finished even as MRSA further developed its dangers...

...so that on that night and again when the US border is closed due to pandemic 5 days later I will find myself asking how many more words phrases diseases epidemics pandemics slow or fast or overwhelming that first sentence will contain before I finish that work...

...dedicated to all the diseases epidemics pandemics slow or fast or overwhelming that one after another over the past 500 years have penetrated the Americas to kill without mercy and often enough backed by human intent still piercing inaccessible corners inhabited by Indigenous peoples...

…while I get to stumble through 65 more days immersed in history in which not to remember in the asphyxiation of George Floyd the great pandemic of racially motivated police violence that 56 years ago killed my father's best friend on Atlantic Avenue in Brooklyn Sam Watso a guy down from Odanak Alanis Obamsawin called Little Sammy Watso when I met her 23 years later the only other person I've ever met who knew the man…

…outside the guys who hung out those years in my mother's living room and him shot by two off duty members of the NYPD for the crime of saying What the fuck or words to that effect and not raising his hands fast enough then dying gut shot 6 weeks later of peritonitis 42 days or thereabouts of growing pain and delirium before his breath was taken away the cops said they thought him a member of the Gallo Gang my brother another good Indian soon to be dead…

…that fall of my 2nd year I think it was though it could have been my 1st at the University of Chicago days when I worked with Friends of SNCC The Student Nonviolent Coordinating Committee that started out building the Civil Rights Movement in the US South by then come north to address more carefully hidden acts of racism Congressman John Lewis once its head now 80 with pancreatic cancer on the demonstration in Washington DC only 3 days ago to protest the exact same issue…

…that I was helping to document that same fall my dad's letter came through going to the homes of African American mothers accompanied by SNCC workers to transcribe testimony about their sons dead at the hands of Chicago cops 3 boys I think 2 maybe in the same family all I remember is a bay window a swollen knuckled dark brown hand sheer lace curtains the sound of crying and talk of a screwdriver taken likely enough on purpose for a knife…

…and then there's my own hand on the cold grey painted tinder block of my dorm room wall as my other hand shakes while holding out in front of me the sheets of yellow lined legal paper containing the excruciatingly lovely loops penned in blue ball point of my dad's

handwriting gained in 6 years of education on his Oklahoma
reservation telling me of Sam's death in NYC before he goes back
out to sea and 9 months around the world sailing ...

...while I will quit university the following spring whichever it is to
start to organize while he's still away against the war in Vietnam a
country from which some trip before he brought me the conical
straw hat with some flowers inside I'll wear to the March on
Washington for Jobs and Freedom that summer of 1963 whose fall
was likely the one before the one that saw Sam killed and so tired
from days of helping organize the New York buses I'll dream under a
tree while MLK talks of his dream still unrealized...

...and 4 years later move to Mexico to be there for the student
movement of 1968 starting in tear gas and the batons of riot police
then ending 69 days full of peaceful demonstrations later in massacre
at the hands of the army that echo far too strongly in the 16 days
since George Floyd's death in threats of when the looting starts the
shooting starts or for that matter before why not bring in the troops
guns at the ready in support of police batons and tear gas that has
grown new power and a gentler name pepper balls they call this new
iteration of irritation to mucus membranes and stomach lining...

...that I seem somehow to smell through the radio as I hear live the
crowd in Lafayette Square being dispersed 8 days after George
Floyd's death as they explode to bring on vomiting along with tears
then smell it again in the footage coming out of Washington as I
reach toward that reality of running people I cannot touch...

...anymore than I can my own past running with people or have in
85 days another human being all the days the years running together
life and history chronicle and story until I do not know from day to
day what is dream and what is nightmare what ends in genocide and
what ends injustice...

Lorna Crozier

The Stars

Years ago, we hosted a poet from Beijing.
Our house was in, what some would call, the country.
Winter on our coast, everything was washed
and washed again by rain, and before we sat at our table,
we invited him, our very honoured guest,
through the sliding glass doors onto the deck
and he looked up. He'd never seen the stars before.
You must be very rich, he said, to live here.
We're only poets, like you, my husband said,
but in Canada, it's not unusual
to see the sky.

When I went to Beijing, five years later,
the woman from the university who met me
at the airport, gave me a mask, for the pollution
she said. On my day off, I walked on my own, the only
woman, the only person, really, without a tour guide,
into the Forbidden City. Some in masks, others not.
Everyone looked at me as if it were I
who was forbidden. I wanted out, not because
of being strange, that is, being alone,
or walking down the stairs in the wrong direction,
a tide of people forcing me back up,
but the crowds, the heat, the air pressed down,
and the ribs holding my heart collapsed.

I think of my friend now at his apartment in Beijing,
a place I was not invited to. This was not unusual,
I found out later. We met at a restaurant,
a bookstore where we read poems together.
The audience was appreciative, and all of them
Chinese. The translations of my poems, a scholar
in the front row told me, were very fine.

This spring, the streets deserted, in many countries
loved ones dying alone in what we here
call *care* homes (my husband died a year ago
of other causes—beside him in the bed I kissed
his head, his chest, his feet) when my Beijing friend
walks outside in one in the biggest cities in the world,
can he can see, for the first time there, the stars?

Roberta Rees

Raw

I

Because we're human
Because thought, emotion, belief, and for some, soul
As if
Taste of a thought on the tongue, lemony as lemon, high-pitched
wild as a falcon's cry
As if soul is sparrow
Spray of blood, bone, feather when falcon talons hit
Or not
Sparrow flit, dive, swoop
Heart racing
Breath fast, shallow

My dying mother's
My fierce loving, tender tough mother
Pre-covid but everything covid to her ravaged lungs
Cold virus, flu virus, scent invisible to the wearer, whiff of detergent,
shampoo, fabric softener, deodorant, essential oil, perfume
Screaming falcon to my mother
Oxygen tethered in her apartment for years
And how can she swerve, swoop, escape
Talons and beaks
Bearing love, bearing innocence, bearing ignorance, bearing death,
bearing down
The gasping, rocking, pounding on her chest, vomiting, hit after hit
of heart racing drug
Her ravaged lungs

Her hand claw thin clutching mine
She rocks, gasps, chokes my name over and over, oh Berta, Berta,
Berta
But when she can, when her lungs can, when voice, her voice, her
story, our story
When 18 years old, weight of West Coast damp on her lungs
In a hospital room, drowning
And her heart, her heart
Her French Metis mother whose lungs, whose heart
Exploded, the doctor said her heart exploded
3 weeks after my mom pulled her 11 year old self from the river
No metaphor, no simile
Gasping, raw flesh, raw bone, blood
Her dying mother's name on her lips
The man who abducted, raped, bit, beat her
Rock in his hand meant for her skull
Her mother on top of a hill – come on, you can make it, you can
make it
And she was running up the hill, chest pounding, Mommy, mommy
And her heart, her heart
The intern on her chest, pounding – come on, you can make it, you
can make it
And the doctor – kind, progressive, debonair, convertible and scarves
Before his convertible crash and wheelchair
Because time and rivers run downslope
Except when lake or ocean
And what was is and will be, all at once

As covid spins us face to face, body to body, with flesh and blood
people, Spanish flu, the great plague, polio, TB, small pox genocide
of Indigenous mothers, fathers, daughters, sons, aunts, uncles,
brothers, sisters, grandmothers, grandfathers, friends, Japanese
internment camps, residential schools

Our own births, physical rawness of our own deaths
The kind, debonair doctor telling my 20 year old meat packing plant
worker father, we'll put her in the sun, bring the baby
My mother's eyes lake green river green coastal
Ocean on her chest, 10 month old baby on her chest
I couldn't die, she says, I was in and out of consciousness, when I
came to with you kissing me I couldn't die

How we could take it for granted
Touch, being with, being there
How we held her hands, lay cold cloths on her head, moistened her
mouth
How she stared into our eyes, our mouths
You can make it, Mom, you can make it

How covid, how virus
How invisible, infectious, transmissible
How holes in lungs
How suffering
How even when it's not covid
But prevention, containment, flattening the curve, protection
As if words

My mother died, a friend says, her voice, face small, far away on my
phone screen
My sister and I couldn't go see her for three months
My mother was afraid and we couldn't be there with her

II

How I want to write
Because we're human
As if humanity
Or the lack of
Respect for the humanity of black life, brown life
As if white superiority, white fragility aren't weapons pulled out in a
park to threaten the life of a black bird watcher

As if the filthy fiction of race were natural as virus
Infecting us into rationalized pandemics of white knees on necks
Stolen children, stolen land
As if we can't hear "I can't breathe I can't breathe"
As if the blood of slaves
As if the bodies of Indigenous women
As if contemporary slave labour
As if immigrant meat packing plant workers
Migrant farm workers
Hospital cleaners
Doctors, nurses
Check out clerks working three jobs
As if we're all feeding our children equally to white power, warning
our daughters, our sons about being shot in the back, being abducted,
brutalized, murdered by systems meant to protect, educate, heal
As if covid 19 kills us all equally
As if skin colour, sex, naturally make us prone to poverty, violence,
injustice
As if we were ever all in this together
As if "that's in the past," "the world isn't like that anymore," "you're
just too sensitive to racism,   sexism, classism," "they should just get
over it,"
As if "help me, mom, god help me" is only human if it's white
Or "I'm afraid to go to work because of this virus, but I have to
because my family will starve"
As if having a black friend, a Chinese niece, a Metis grandmother
erases white privilege
As if whiteness isn't an anti-black, anti-brown construct
As if whiteness isn't power
As if wealthy white maleness isn't eating the world
As if admitting white privilege will eat holes in our lungs
As if empathy, responsibility, systemic change, institutional change
will break our white necks

III

How I want to focus on birds for being birds
The black-capped chickadees flitting into the hollow of our crab
apple tree
Silvery slivery chirp of baby birds wide beaked
Except for magpies beaking the back legs off baby jackrabbits
Gut splitting screams

Human hubris and the narrative mind
Crashing in waves
Viral waves, first wave second wave third wave
Washed off our feet, crashed upside down
Heart racing, choking on fear, on hope
Covid naked, salt stung, ears and eyes open

Rosemary Griebel

Pandemus

The church bells stopped.
We sat in our rooms and looked out
on silent streets.
At first it was hard.
The greyness of March,
dusky mornings and sallow sleet.
Each day so much like the other
except for the growing tally
of sick and dead.
Some of us turned to history and read
about the black plague.
It could be worse, we said.
Some of us couldn't sleep.
Some died alone.
We moved like ghosts
through food stores
carrying tin cans
and toilet paper.
Thick throated, we shouted
through windows, across blue screens.
Our hands and mouths
were weapons,
and we ached for touch.

When spring arrived
Noli Timere
was scrawled on the fence
in front of the homeless shelter.
The air filled with birdsong,
and the corona of sun
goldened the gardens.
The green ribs of the river
exhaled, feeding fish and flies
weeds and light.
In the streets face masks
scattered like love notes.
We longed for change,
imagined a new order
and kinder power.
Sickness scoured
the city, scoured the globe.
Yet the stench
of wrongdoing remained.

Pamela Medland

The Plunge

You sway on the faultline
prepared, you say, to fall.
But already your breath is laboured,
it will be a swimming into death,
a drowning.

There's no easy way to cross
the threshold, but still,
a fight for breath is violent,
a knife in the lungs—
the tearing away of words
that could have been said.

I sway with you as we wait
for the wave that will take you.
We both know I'll pull back,
release your hand at the last moment,
let you flail alone against the tide.

Micheline Maylor

The Great Amplification Fugue

Your life, never so real. Look. Here is what you built.
This saggy-ass, dumpy comfort zone frump. Pandemic
blue. Here is who you live with, this is what you think,
what you do all day, this home you made. Question
What will you make tomorrow? Tomorrow
never comes. It's all here, now. Amplified. The river
too, gleams an array of molecules just once,
that occurrence of sound wavering just once. Like this.
Just time but again and forward again. Grey-gone
and down to the other town. How sent we are to other
places even in the right here right now/now. Mind
wandering children sent into mornings of lost sweaters,
yin poses on the dewy ground while some wandering star
gleams inside the anxiety box of the heart/caged
animal calls itself light and why try to catch it?
It's all here, now, and perfect, there's just this, amplified,
and this is what you built and the water just runs,
and if you listen you hear it too, in the studs of your house,
the trickle/in the digits of your bank balance,
this is what you built, what you accumulated. It's all
in perfect motion to the town down-stream, where snakes
live in knots beside your mother's river house. This is
the house you built. This is the crumbling house that falls
to sand to nothing but silt in the river. Remember this
is your illusion, your daydream in your pajamas. Your
very own virus dream. Your own tight white light caught
in your retina. This is your seeing that goes like a raft into
the river of time. There is no time. There is nothing but here,
now, wet. Glistening and loud and amplified. Now, and perfect.

Elizabeth Greene

Land of No Shadow

Grey day after day,
streets empty, stores close.
Spring marked by
absence of hyacinths
in my living room.

Outside
a few bursts of transforming sun
promise a different season,

but for now,
this stillness, this chill,
this threat of virus
from the air,
this is history.

May steals reluctantly into leaf.
Crocuses, daffodils surge skyward
as if this month was normal.

Seven sleek fox kits
lithe, bright russet,
venture from their lair.

Birds chatter and swoop.
The earth is healing.
You can feel her breathe.

In these times
the Fates clip life threads
short and fast.

The virus settles into lungs.
Nine minutes of a cop's knee
on George Floyd's neck

sever his life,
though not without surges
of grief, rage, protest.

The world bursts into the streets,
some armed, some chanting.
In this disease, this anger,

this grief, this turbulence, these people
in the streets, in this uncertainty,
a new age forms.

Diana Manole

Shrimp Fried Rice with a Hint of Saffron

The phone rings at midnight—
heart attack, funeral in two days, too hot to wait any longer.
She grips her pendant, the rice grain on which grandpa
wrote her name when she was born—
borders still closed, countries like bird cages forsaking flight,
she falls back to sleep dreaming
of sheep with glass bells surrounding her at Pearson airport.

When she finishes her evening shift at the
Real Canadian Superstore
over there it's already the time to lay him to rest—
professional wailers howl around the coffin,
uncles, aunts, and neighbours nod "He was a good man!"
mom bites her nails, wondering if she turned off the oven
before leaving,
cemetery beggars circle at a respectful distance, ready to race
for the goodie bags—
packed meals, soul cakes included, given away to keep the dead
nourished on his way,
the end of the funeral service coincides with the TTC night bus finally
arriving.

She cooks shrimp fried rice with a hint of saffron—
grandpa's favourite when he still owned a restaurant.

Grain swell, starch empathy bubbling in the pot,
bean sprouts and green onions wriggle covered
in soy sauce as if an echo of the Cultural Revolution gore
and wounds,
she stirs
her present and his past
till all is smoothly blended just as the family *over there* gathers
for the wake—
words dipped in coconut oil, tears watering down the wine,
quick prayers between dishes,
mom hastily washing dinner plates for the newly arrived,
pain's a luxury when the house's full,
a burden when you mourn alone,
over there they hum *Ave Maria*, arms braided
over each other's shoulders like dough,
over here she rushes to the back alley behind *The Jester on Yonge*
(founded 1989, bankrupt by COVID-19, May 2020)
where a red-haired, blue-eyed, middle-aged man
lives in a cardboard hut
with his bike and his rescue dog
a lit candle, which he blows out crossing himself,
shrimps on top like pink rosebuds
rewriting her name on rice.

Ellie Sawatzky

Aubade at the End of the World

4am

      in your friends' house
      our love wakes their baby

the trilingual

      cat understands the hum
      of our animal tongues

bells

      clang an alarm
      for the airport

sounding

      our fleeting separation my departure
      from this year to the next

what could be

      any kind of year because
      it hasn't happened yet

you and I

      we only just happened
      we can't see

the beginning

      your grandmother's ashes
      sprinkled on the pink ice

of the river

      we can't ask what's
      on the other side

— 2019/2020

Lea Harper

Swan Song

For LG

Life is terminal. Given its expiry date
you refuse agony, choose dignity
to greet the unknown, face to face.

In the time of Covid there are no intimate goodbyes
no hearse to lead the procession.

You choose to go gently, with a fond farewell
to attend your funeral from a *safe distance.*
The slow cavalcade of cars past your house--
a wave of signs, the shape of a heart, a rainbow, the words *we love you.*
We lean through open windows, unmasked, that you might see us truly
one last time, from the roadside where you stand, smiling,
hands crossed at your breast.

So much begins and ends with a circle of friends
women who remember how to weep and rejoice
a choir learning to sing in one voice,
reshape the world. Even now,
your vibrato soars above us:
My heart is moved by all I cannot save . . .

Behind you, in sharp relief, the sun releases its last burst of energy
on the flat line of horizon. How beautiful and valiant
the force of nature, the clear-eyed vision:
A woman in her fullness, in the final throes of labour
knowing she's exactly where she needs to be,
that her work is almost done, surrenders.

You choose to leave with grace.
You choose to go simply.
Choose to simply go.

My Heart is Moved, from the Dream of a Common Language by
Adrienne Rich.
Music by Carolyn Dade, sung by the Outloud Women's choir of
Haliburton

Resilience and Reverie

Cecelia Frey

When was it we learned to live together?

was it that night

you threw up down your coat sleeve which

possibly was the night of the conception

of our first born.

or was it the morning we saw our last son

off to school, his tawny polished face and

combed hair and spanky new runners that flashed

and

I turned back into an empty house

and you

or when our oldest moved out and that was the beginning

of what they call the empty nest syndrome although

they kept coming back

and in between left reminders

record collections and sound equipment beneath the stairs

notebooks of algorithms and perfect math

and tapes and disks and games and xmas decorations

but the day did come when the last one left

and we had to face each other

down what seemed a very long dinner table and

it was suddenly very quiet

or when you retired and there you were

with the fridge door opening at strange intervals

and your solution to every crisis or even non crisis

going out into the back yard

and hammering

something or sawing and

on the other side of the window my hand hovering

above the keyboard about to drop for the kill

on the crucial word for the perfect sentence and suddenly

the whine of the power saw and the word fled forever

and the world lost that perfect sentence

or nearly sixty years on

om that party (whose was it anyway?)

locked together in the solitary of an epidemic pandemic

without buffer of family and friends

will we learn to live together now?

two old heads bent over the dining room table

and fifteen hundred jigsaw puzzle pieces

that look so small after decades of large pieces

of little puzzles for six-year-olds

and I

don't mess with the bit you're working on because

I know how you hate that

and when we walk in the park

keeping social distance, six feet or 2.2 metres

you walk ahead and turn at intervals

to see if I'm keeping up

and if I'm not you stop and wait

but some days I'm in the lead

and then it's my turn to turn

and wait for you and in this way

we amble and shamble along the path

and I think maybe now

we have finally got the hang of this living together.

Beth Everest

for Emily

it's her birthday
my daughter
she sends a text – a photo:
I can't see her face
under the shield. hood, gown, gloves
on my way in the text says. she
& the 2 other medical residents
cover the next back to back to back
shifts

then the 2nd photo
& I forget to breathe: for her
the change is perhaps gradual
a change because of what she does & what she sees; for me
it happens like a photographic flash, the image
that remains long after the pupils squeeze
shut.
her face
drawn older
than her 27 years, it's not just what we read
in the news or the puffy sweat pale of
the intubations, dyspnea,
lack of respirators, cytokine storms
the thefts of PPEs, the overdoses, deaths or even
when she tells me that after midnight, the whole
busload of patients from the shelter all covid+
who have no place to go & she
has nowhere to put them but hospital hallways
or the other, a young patient injecting his own
feces to prolong an infection, him too terrified to keep
living on the street

it's her eyes:
what I see & what
I cannot unsee, cannot unhear
even speaking hitches in my throat.
my daughter's blood black eyes
I cannot look or look away or listen to her voice
rising from the printed word, the text, the photo,
her mouth, her lips
thin
flat line

Sandra Sugimoto

"Clearly Speaking"

3 pm, Nigel —
emphatic gestures transcend
interpretation

Images: video stills from CTV live update, March 24, 2020/Nigel Howard interpreting for Dr. Bonnie Henry.

Weyman Chan

Spring Song for Friday March 13, 2020

Silly trip up one's fragile equilibrium on
whodunits just when Thunberg
was starting to kick up the big boys' sandbox
there are no planes overhead but this morning
northern flickers gawped from a skeletal lilac
on my walk to work where I was stopped at Emerg

       showed my badge got my forehead irradiated to measure
       fever & thought I heard lungs sickened
then quiet as they made their way to open sky

       earthworms love stygian vegetables they
       are dark tools & eating them the Chinese say will help you
breathe while doctors elsewhere bring in their own ski masks
for the unprecedented shortage of masks is such
that what I'd seen before can't
sort its white coat from the graph
       speeding to beat the contact
       traceable bio
       surface marker that'll stop our bottomless eyes

if I could pretend I'm
short of breath & not be lachrymose about it
would fasting while flagellating garlic hallucinate me a new normal?
try hollowed out normal or my-fetus-is-screwed normal

       down goes my pandemicky penny stock
    nosediving pulse-ox
   oops pardon my earthworms for writhing at
meme trauma when Teresa Tam's jitters
       re-tweet sunshine

treaty grass my feet can't
feel & everyone's on Zoom being outré I suppose
about how it all went down
  first monkey meat to human now bat to
  pangolin just leave the fucking jungle alone

no one sings alone from their perch nor
do ventilators tighten the bag over your head
steaming up your eyes

should Skynet or anti-vaxxers lead with
signage at the gates NO
HAND SANITIZER REEQUIRED when holding the door open
for fellow travellers

everyone wants happy
messaging
earthworms needn't sorrow at the beak's last peck

    nor tarry the chthonic drip of Nurse Smiley
    when I don that N95 for one more sole mio

Yasmin Ladha

"Us"

Bella ciao! Bella ciao! Applause from filigreed balconies.
The dancer bows. His dangling shopping bag, a grave
reminder. When pots clang, a bit of *du'a,* a bit of psalm
comes out of our mouths. *Turn your ear to me.* Parlor
lipstick forgotten, we clang and clang unvarnished
thanks to the saviors in scrubs. The god with the inky
blue throat drank all the poison in the oceans. Not for
a florist's glossy ribbons or the pernickety questions of
the barista, the god drank hazmat without fanfare. A
loner, and of shameless manners, he did not get along
with his father-in-law. No, he will not woo us. A
lobster grew a Pepsi claw. We carried on. Coral
etiolated. Penguins. The seabird. We carried on. And
malicious to our own. A spoonful of sugar makes the
disinfectant go down. Home, hundreds of kilometers
away, the fools asleep on the railway tracks. A train
comes along. Destiny's greeting, "Contact with the
train or pneumothorax?" Not your downcast eyes,
Shiv, not now. *You know, you know,* we rise out of taint,
shamans and healers, stout round table sharers. The
muezzin's full throttle *azan,* bereft. 40 days passed.
The number that once was, today, sweeter than a boon;
now days into weeks into months, maybe years.
Timorous prayers, but our love, sound as Cordelia's.
The nurse comes a-flying. Wings and masked, arms
lifted. She will keep our soul. White supper plates, a
jug of water, even the dreaded pink slip, our inbuilt
fortifiers. This time, pink notices scotch-taped onto
store doors. *There, there.* We know how to pick up
from here. I have a nightmare that my beloved is
having an affair. Mummy napping beside me. Is this
my black bordered envelope? She is ninety, in Calgary.

Cap in hand, or the bully, or will we all share the
nectar? Stout shamans we are, but quicksilver with
lessons.   Are the gods scoffing? Buildings stand, the
grass is green... *tu*, my affectionate one; *tu*, my clement
one; *tu*, my guard; stay awhile, stay until I finish my *pain
au chocolat*.

A cyclist pedals past. An ordinary activity, glittery as
Cinderella in her carriage of gold. *There, there*. In
Muscat's 37 °C, I smell Calgary's mulchy moist gardens
of May. The prime minister drenches the refugees,
"You're home!" Is he a round table psycho or the
perfect gardener, hueing the airport rampant? Myrrh
and frankincense. (*In Arabia, I have run out of perfume.
Go figure.*) Hello, Tommy Douglas.   Hello, shelf-
stacker. A poet from the interior brings me freshly
harvested Omani garlic, the grandee of panaceas. I
head downstairs, raisin loaf still too hot and his
thermos of coffee for the road (*a prairie thing to do*).
Garlic, pink as fingernails, to fight the pox. In the
briefest pow-wow amidst shuttered shops, every bit of
love pressed in deep and swift. From a top window, a
woman watches. *Bella ciao*. The three of us.

Love and Laughter

Sheri-D Wilson

Love in the Time of Corona

Our faces have changed
and we don't yet know, what we look like,
as we search for a new way
to live and love

We oscillate between
paralysis, monotony and flow,
wonder if we will ever wake
from this CoVid coma, if we will ever
know anything again, wonder
if we will only be able to dream –
of trips to far-off places,
sitting in stands cheering,
standing O's for virtuoso's,
or dancing wild to Motown live
on a Sunday afternoon

Time changed places with space
and dissolved, along
with the high paced rat race
of our lives – postponed
indefinitely, cancelled –
later is the new now,
re: zoom, push the reset button
every time we make an expedition
into the outside world,
zone out, reel, try to keep it real
too real to feel – it's unreal –

To tell you the truth
it took a pandemic for me to learn
to bake a loaf of banana bread – yes
I found Grandma Nian's recipe,
fashioned the facsimile of a loaf pan,
the wrong shape, it turned out
the right taste, each bite of banana bread
reminded me of her, each bite
brought me closer to her
and the memory of sweeter occasions –
a beautiful boon at a time when
the only way to touch someone
is in their heart,
to be touched by tenderness
heart to heart

There will always be another ski pass
another hill, another slope, breath of fresh air,
after the age of asphyxiation and despair
is behind us – we wonder
what will become a thing of the past?

Maybe we'll become more human
as the earth takes a moment to breathe,
as the earth takes a moment to breathe,
we wash our hands raw, wear homemade masks,
try to learn the perfect distance
that might save our own breath,
and one day we might fill
that empty space, with the beauty
of a sunset, instead of a pending death,
six feet above to avoid six feet below

One thing's for certain,
I had no idea I touched myself so much
hand to hair, sweeping it back
fingers to face, nose, and lips,
adjusting glasses, and the arid eclipse
to remove sleep from my eyes –

Some days I just break down and cry
grieving the life I once had, now gone
along with hugs and kisses, shaking hands
freedoms, and long good-byes

Or those nights when I wake
with a little cough, a slight headache
and I think I caught it somehow
in isolation – that it's the end,
and I spend the rest of the night in a cold sweat
in a deep tête-à-tête with death,
that's when my heart goes out to the people
on the front lines, the ones taking care

On those days, and after those nights
the only thing that comforts me
is a potato – I know, it sounds trite
but sometimes the only thing
that will lift my spirit
is scalloped potatoes, spuds

I think of my other Grandma, the poet
who arrived here from Ireland
with five cents and a dream of love
in her pocket – when she went to spirit
all her writing was lost, scattered
to the earth, and all that was left
was a locket, with a small strand
of her hair

Today, I follow her dream
and turn to the face of love—
today, as I perform a wedding
in this time of social distance,
my voice breaks
on the front lawn
under the weeping willow,
about to bloom in yellow catkins

My voice breaks with the blight of beauty
at the love I see standing before me
beneath long feathery branches
over moonstone roots

A young couple ties the knot,
handfasting at a distance
they bind their own hands
in the ancestral light, of fertility sighs
in this time of pandemic,
they speak the vows of their souls
in a creation divination
that humbles, that extols

My body holds back tears,
as I wed them from afar, I am struck
by the closeness of their hearts
the first real day of spring

They are beaming
global ghosts into dancing light
it swirls around them,
and the word corona
returns to its original meaning
aurora borealis, solar soma
overhead, their light
is likened to a crown,
and I say to them,
"you may kiss with joy"

Paulette Dubé

the light was just starting

the light was just starting as we skied

(Raymond glided, I shuffled)

over Pyramid Lake you could pick any direction - blue sky over here

cloudy and windy over there

it was as though you could decide

what to see

almost like you had the choice

of how you were going to feel

I drive along in my skin suit

and realise the challenge ahead

is to sustain this feeling, like falling in love.

Right now, oooooh! this is (a) bad (boy) but I can do this

I can make poetry, cookies, be creative and passionate, vociferous,

anxious, giddy, extreme, compassionate, empathetic, joy filled and

and

tomorrow, I need to be able to do it again.

Lucky I am not so much a race car driver as a long-haul trucker

How to call a whale -
put you ear next to a wall
the Library of Alexandria say, or the Wailing Wall in Jerusalem
that Douglas fir on the ridge will do
put your arms around an elk and bury
your face in her flank if that's all you have
practice walking on tiptoes, stooped over
practice rumbling your spleen and your liver
until you wander salty as tears, filled with krill and your mother's face
the one who could cut an apple in the palm of her hand
and knew all the important phone numbers by heart.

In a world of sharp, urgent noise where words stopped making
sense, I was found lacking.
In nature I am whole, because that is how I find that place.

two pieces of the sky flew onto a branch with a soft shweep
the branch easily held those sky-blue pieces

when the sky chooses to fall completely

a soft shweep will sing our passing

John Barton

Virus Daybook

We stand in vigil, lined up famine-style
Compiling shopping lists to archive tastes
Doubtless to carry forward, the culled aisles
Called on to be provisioned a foretaste

Of crushed sightings of unshelved tomatoes
And fished-out runs on endangered tuna
Our carts skittering past, forced to our toes
Till, too late, what's there's still gone, lacunas

Our survival skills can't fill, draft online
FAQs doping our game, rota of symptoms
Weighed against what listlessness undermines
Obliged to mete out distance, unwelcome

While we wait, the stillness inside the store
Unwonted, so unwanted what's in store.

    ●

Unwonted, so unwanted what's in store
We self-isolate, having washed our hands
Not just of germs, but the germ of cocksure
Unguarded entanglements, such demands

A contagion staggering the planet
All of desire put aside with the bleach
Beneath the sink, want called to the carpet
And judged, ignored stains unimpeachable

What we've spilt covertly starting to spread
Promiscuous conviviality
An import bottled in lovers and friends
If opened hard to cork, reality

Better spent with long books and meals for one
The yen for intimacy overcome.

•

The yen for intimacy overcome
Our solitary walks salutary
Streets quiet despite those who outrun us
Jogging toward their obituaries

At unsafe, uneven speeds, their exhale
A butterfly net they ensnare us with
Incurably—our lungs wings they outsail—
Till they wind us, freed to sunbathe or seethe

Our salutary walks solitary
Along harbours so static they mirror
Vacated worlds upside-down, boat-empty
Freeze-framed, unreflective, no wavy blur

Should a flock of geese alight on itself
Cold, companionable, constant, aloof.

•

Cold, companionable, constant, aloof
The man smoking all day across from me
Scatters ash from his balcony, stormproof
Windows behind him enduring calmly

Rays of spring sun, elbows bent to the rail
So often he overshadows my thoughts

While reading, making senseless without fail
This subterfuge, how feeling safe is fraught

But, glancing up, I find I like him there
The nearest I'm allowed a confidant
One who can keep his distance while caring
In no way for me, smoking in private

He thinks, blind to how I watch from afar
The complicit sun leaving us unmarred.

•

The complicit sun leaving us unmarred
I step outside with my isolation
The labyrinth gate I walk to left ajar
Below limbs of wind-struck cherry to shun

Sundry vectors of unreasoned panic
Luring me no deeper in till let go
The scattering petals epiphanic
Their mandala a gyre I set aglow

Circling in and about, around and out
The self-effacing path the rock shards mark
Level with the mown grass, a walkabout
To rake me flat under sky in this park

Seldom as in the pink of loneliness
Empathy made pivotal through crisis.

•

Empathy made pivotal through crisis
The coins shops fear are septic I offer
To a tall, cold-looking man I'm sure is
Penniless, change routinely spent proffered

To feed my conscience, help it assure more
Stomachs stay full because all hearts rest less
Empty of distress, my scruples before
Today not replete, the streets I walk blessed

Although void of commerce to intersect
Like minds joined together haphazardly
Despite what distance obliges, unchecked
Viral spread stepped around straightforwardly

Conviction at arm's length somehow heightened
A pandemic of unconcern flattened.

•

A pandemic of unconcern flattened
The door to this solace we'd not wanted
Locking behind us for like days on end
Worlds within world, by patience undaunted

If rendered claustrophobic, outside views
Turned inward, an internal exile, pride
A quiet scrubbed of exhaustion, renewed
By reserve, a heron or gull biding

Its time to be anywhere I am not
Freed by my absence, fountains in the square
Their fitful spray uninspired, overshot
By night skies more starry, daytimes more clear

All the while, my appetites undefiled
We stand in vigil, lined up famine-style.

Lori M. Feldberg

Covid at the Grocery Store

Read with a snappy swinging rhythm!

Stand yourself in line
Two meters apart
Adjust your mask
And wait, wait, wait
Move up the line
Move up again
And so it all goes
Until you're inside

Wipe down your cart
Wipe off your hands
Follow the arrows
And don't step behind
Don't squeeze the produce
Don't dare lean close
Don't sniff that stuff
Take what you touch

No time for labels
Search high and low
Next time you'll find it
Move. Move some more
Head down next aisle
Hey! Wrong way, dude!
Gotta face the shelves
And side-step around

"Stop!" the floor reads
Oops, the wrong way
See what you want
Can't go there
Hurry your choices
Do a grid search
Back to other aisle
Get what you wanted

Reach store's far side
Someone dithering
Wait and wait some more
Fin ... al ... ly!
Now, where's line's end?
Way down there
Two meters apart
Move. Move up some more

Arrive at the till
Just keep your distance
Step up for your turn
Hurry to unload
Move behind the shield
Hold out shopping card
Give up your payment
Quick pack your bags up

Double quick-trot out
Someone behind
Rush out the door
Over to the car
Unload and return
You're still in high gear
Wipe down your cart
Wipe off your hands

Back to the car
Alone at last
Remove your mask
Breeeeathe … loooong
Gotta get home
Unpack, wash down
'nother week gone
In Covid time!

Kim Goldberg

Let's Pretend

Let's pretend we are in the Before time
When we clustered like lemurs at the bakery
Tasting each other's tarts and meringue
Let's pretend we are in the Before time
For this game we must use our pataphysical minds
I can tongue your éclair with some fakery
Let's pretend we are in the Before time
And cluster like lemurs at the bakery

Esther Sokolov Fine

At the End of the Day

We are all paying a price
as we go the extra mile
on the same path
    we have your back.

We're all in this together
nothing is off the tunnel,
everything's on the bubble
    there's light at the end of the table.

A tip of the iceberg
cracks through the falls,
whatever it takes
    not yet out of the water.

Second wave,
no green light
no playbook.
    Firing on all sides

the buck stops here
all hands on deck
full steam ahead
    full head of steam

on the ground
together we are stronger
there's nothing we can't do.
    We should hold our heads high

full support
in these dark times
sparing no expense
    to get through this together

more help is on the way.
Light at the end of the tunnel
at the end of the day:
     which end?

What spreads faster the Pandemic virus or the Pandemic clichés?
     It's anti-body's guess.

Ray McGinnis

For Self's Sake

At dawn I open self eyes, self step
toward the sink, self splash myself,
self brush self teeth, self apply face cream.
Self rinse off self. Me, myself, and I
self step down the hall to the kitchen.
Listen to news about an <u>Amazon.com</u> warehouse fire,
employees "self-evacuating,"
and the daily count.

I self boil the kettle, self measure coffee,
self set the table myself. I self taste
each spoon of granola. I self swallow.
Self smile. Self contemplate a bird flying by.
Self sip one more sip. Self turn
on the computer. Self look for a word.
All by myself, I self-isolate.

Self consider "self evacuating," "self-isolating,"
"self-distancing," self-consciousness, self-disclosure,
self explaining, self approaching, self reproaching,
self sequestering, self segregating, self seclusion,
self connecting, self mingling, self integrating,
self abandoning, self decamping, self skidaddling,
self marketing, self-publishing, self-abasing,
self-actualizing, self-admiration, self-analyzing,
self-assessment, self-adhesive, self-appointment,
self-awareness, self-abnegation, self-assurance,
self-importance, self-portraiture, self-possession,
self-indulgence, self-explanatory, the self-employed,
self-begotten, self-centering, self-certification,
self-concerned, self-confidence, self-congratulatory,
self-censorship, self-contempt, self-control,

self-criticism, self-definition, self-deprecation,
self-destructiveness, self-determination, self-differentiation,
self-discipline, self-esteem, self-evident,
self-help, self-expression, self-finance,
self-flagellation, self-flattery, self-fulfilling,
self-generating, self-glorification, self-gratification,
self-hatred, self-hypnosis, self-identification,
self-involved, self-justifying, self-limitation,
self-loathing, self-made, self-motivated,
self-mutilation, self-opinionatedness, self-parodying,
self-pitying, self-possession, self-preservation,
self-realization, self-reflection, self-respect,
self-restraint, self-revealing, self-sacrifice,
self-satisfaction, self-selection, self-stimulation,
self-supporting, self-sustaining, self-taught,
self-torment, self-transcendence, self-worth,
self-righteous, selfsame, self-service,
self absorbing, selflessness, selfishness, self exculpate,
self impeach, self clemency, Saint Clement.

All for self's sake, I take a selfie.
Self-satisfied.

Leslie Y. Dawson

Pandemic Plumbing

Always Plumbing and Heating sent me an email.
They promised to wash their hands and wear booties
when they came to clear out my clogged toilet
or fix my furnace.
They will lay down their tools on a special red carpet
and stay home if they're sick.

While the whole world is shutting down
toilets still get clogged
pipes burst in the cold
and pilot lights go out.

Rejoice!
Plumbers are still on the job!

I like the idea
of a plumber coming to my door
knocking loudly
carrying a box of tools to fix something.
The whole idea of *fixing* something
makes me happy.
A problem like a clogged toilet
could be a blessing
a problem so discrete, so manageable,
that you can call for help
and someone will come.

It's not the end of the world after all.
Six onions were left in the store this afternoon
and a few bags of rice.
I'm not panicking. There will be more onions tomorrow
and if my sink backs up
I can still call *Always Plumbing and Heating.*

Adrienne Drobnies

Food and Drink

Now we make our inventories
just as our grandparents did
during deprivation, Depression, war

Stocks of dried beans
frozen breads and baked goods
counting cans with fingertips
and careful measure

Now we make our inventories –
mental and material –
dinners, lunches and breakfasts,
the beer, wine and liquor

Words newly known and newly
minted – fomites and quarantinis
on line means and meaning
Zoom and Facetime and Skype

Now we make our inventories
of places we won't go
and people we cannot touch
of how much we have hoarded
and squandered

Of the arts made by each plague
Macbeth and *The Ship of Fools*
how much we have lived
and how much we have wasted

Now we take our inventories
of the miracles we have missed and seen
of crows in the evening light off to the rookery
of rainbows that stopped us in our tracks
and blood-dyed sunsets

Of risk and time and how much
we have left

Laurie MacFayden

Seasons

Skinny kids roll past on skinny skateboards
There is time to reflect, to repair, to spend too long in a reclining chair
I have my bed, my view of the sea, *and my poetry to protect me*
I have my well-stocked fridge, I have my books
I care not about my looks.

Through the front window the seasons come and go.
But do they even exist when you cannot be inside of them, outside?
If a tree falls in the pandemic, does anybody
Look up from their laptop?
It's been months of trying to occupy wild, restless hands
Months waiting for the dough to rise,
Banana loaf to bake, tulips to bloom
Months of staring numbly out windows
Wondering why the birds continue warbling,
Don't they know what's happening?
Don't they know we're living in cliché land?
Don't they know *Life as we know it...*
Out the other side...
When this is behind us...

We measure out our lives in streaming episodes.
Months without shaking hands, embracing, human touch abolished
Baking the bread but forbidden from breaking it
With anyone outside your pod
Months of plans spoiled and pots banged,
Lethargy and meditations
Online concerts, invisible caskets.

A few months more will bring autumn again
And what besides the colours of the leaves will have changed?
I'll still be painting my anxiety as a monster.

Alison Dyer

May.31.2020 Pandemic Time

Like carving through the thorny skin of a durian fruit, then slicing
       the creamy, soft, vulnerable flesh inside
Like opening an accordion, and never stopping
Like reaching deep inside a grandparent's memory and making it
       your own
Like knowing Paleozoic time, really knowing it
Like remembering what you didn't do
Like forgetting what you... forgot
Like thinking you'd forgotten something, or maybe hadn't, or maybe
       had, or just maybe…
Like testing quicksand all around, wondering which foot to put where
Like trying to remember the before
Like listening to your heart beat, was it always that offbeat?
Like going into a room and forgetting what for
Like wanting to drink until oblivion's arms take over
Like feeling what love was, and then it was gone.

Contributors Bios

Tanja Bartel's first collection of poetry, *Everyone at This Party* (icehouse poetry/Goose Lane Editions), was released at the beginning of the pandemic in 2020. She lives in Pitt Meadows, BC.

Brian Bartlett, a resident of Halifax since 1990, has published six collections and six chapbooks of poetry and two books of nature writing, as well as compilation of his prose about poetry. He has also edited selected volumes of works by several poets, along with *Collected Poems of Alden Nowlan*.

John Barton's most recent books are a book of poems, *Lost Family: A Memoir* (Signal Editions, 2020) and *The Essential Derk Wynand* (The Porcupine's Quill, 2020). He lives in Victoria, B.C., where he is the city's fifth poet laureate.

Jocko Benoit is the author of three collections of poetry, the latest of which is *Real Estate Deals of the Apocalypse: Poems About Donald Trump*. He is a Canadian living in Washington, DC.

Moni Brar gratefully divides her time between Treaty 7 land and the land of the Syilx of the Okanagan Nation. She is a Punjabi, Sikh Canadian writer exploring diasporan guilt, cultural oppression, intergenerational trauma, and the possibility of healing through literature.

Chris Bullock retired from his career as an English professor at the University of Alberta in 2000, and moved to Vancouver Island. Since then he has published three detective novels jointly with his wife, Kay Stewart, and currently runs a poetry and song circle in Victoria.

Tania Carter has an MA in theatre and a BA in World Literature. Her earliest most significant education was potlatch and a home full of avid readers. She has a beautiful daughter and now resides in Vancouver, BC, where she was born. Tania is focused on longhouse tradition and nature.

Carol Casey lives in Blyth, Ontario, Canada. Her work has been nominated for the Pushcart Prize and has appeared in *The Leaf, The Prairie Journal, Synaeresis* and other online and print publications, including a number of anthologies, most recently, *Much Madness, Divinest Sense, Tending the Fire* and *i am what becomes of broken branch*.

Weyman Chan's *Noise From the Laundry* was a finalist for the 2008 Governor General's Award for poetry. Spotted in Calgary with Heisenberg & Faraday, cat cohorts overseeing his sixth opus.

George Elliott Clarke is the 4th Poet Laureate of Toronto (2012-15) and the 7th Parliamentary (Canadian) Poet Laureate (2016-17). He has books of poetry in Chinese, Italian, and Romanian translation. A native Nova Scotian Afro-Metis, the poet teaches at the University of Toronto, and lives in its host city.

Dennis Cooley is a Winnipeg poet, who has authored 19 books of poetry.

Joan Crate taught English Literature and Creative Writing at Red Deer College for 19 years and now lives in Calgary. Over the years she has been shortlisted for, placed in, or won several awards including the Commonwealth Book Award for Canada, the Bliss Carmen Award for poetry and the W.O. Mitchell Book Award.

Lorna Crozier is a Governor-General Award winner, the author of 18 books of poetry, and an Officer of the Order of Canada, Lorna Crozier lives on Vancouver Island. *Through the Garden: A Love Story (with Cats)*, the story of her life with the writer Patrick Lane, will be published in the fall of 2020.

Leslie Y. Dawson is a retired science reporter, now writing poetry in Edmonton Alberta. She has been writing a poem a day since the beginning of the pandemic.

Brian Day has published four books of poetry with Guernica Editions, including *Conjuring Jesus* and *The Daring of Paradise*. He lives on Salt Spring Island, B.C.

Adrienne Drobnies is a poet from Vancouver, BC whose first book of poetry *Salt and Ashes* (Signature Editions) was published in 2019. She won the Gwendolyn MacEwen Award and was a finalist for the CBC literary prize.

Paulette Dubé lives and works in Jasper, Alberta. Her poetry and prose are based on life, so far.

Alison Dyer won the 2019 Newfoundland & Labrador Book Award for poetry for her debut poetry collection, I'd Write the Sea Like a Parlour Game, (Breakwater Books, 2017). Originally from England and now living in Newfoundland, Dyer has a M.Sc. in physical geography and works as an organic farmer, forager and freelance writer.

Sarah Ens is a writer and editor based in Treaty 1 territory (Winnipeg, Manitoba). In 2019, she won *The New Quarterly*'s Edna Staebler Personal Essay Contest and in the spring of 2020, her debut collection of poetry, *The World Is Mostly Sky*, came out with Turnstone Press.

Beth Everest is a Calgary-based writer whose most recent book Silent Sister: the mastectomy poems won the ABPA Robert Kroetsch award.

Lori Feldberg is a long time writer in many genres. She hails from Central Alberta and enjoys travelling. In the past her books have included her adventures of working on farms in New Zealand and Australia. Humor seems to find its way into nearly everything she writes, including her poetry.

Esther Sokolov Fine is an award winning author of fiction, poetry, essays, academic books and journal articles. She lives in Toronto, where she taught at York University in the Faculty of Education until her retirement in 2015.

Doris Fiszer lives in Ottawa, Ontario and is the winner of the 2017 John Newlove Award and author of two chapbooks: *The Binders,* which won Tree Press's 2016 Chapbook Award and *Sasanka (Wild Flower)* Bywords Publication, 2018. She has recently published her first full-length poetry collection, *Locked in Different Alphabets,* Silver Bow Publishing.

Ian FitzGerald teaches at Alberta University of the Arts in Calgary, Alberta. He has trifled with poetry since teenage and is getting dangerously close to thinking he should take it seriously.

Kate Marshall Flaherty was shortlisted for Arc's "Poem of the Year" 2019, and Exile's Gwendolyn MacEwen Poetry Prize 2018. Her latest poetry book, "Radiant," launched in 2019 in Ontario, where she lives, hikes, canoes and loves to write.

Cecelia Frey, who lives and writes in Calgary, is a past recipient of the Writers' Guild of Alberta Golden Pen Award. Her latest books are Lovers Fall Back to Earth (fiction, 2018) and North (poetry, 2017).

Donna Friesen is an expressive arts facilitator and former lawyer who resides in Calgary, Alberta. She writes poetry as a way of engaging more deeply with the many layers of her life.

Myrna Garanis lives on a pie-shaped block in Edmonton, reason enough for co-editing with Ivan Sundal the *Life of Pie: prairie poems and prose* this pandemic spring.

Tea Gerbeza (she/her) is a disabled poet and paper quilling artist from Treaty 4 territory (Regina, Saskatchewan). Her poems have won an Honourable Mention in the 2019 Short *Grain* Contest. You can find Tea's most recent work in *antilang., the Society,* and *Spring*

Kim Goldberg is the author of eight books of poetry and nonfiction including most recently *Devolution,* poems of ecopocalypse, from Caitlin Press. She lives in Nanaimo, BC.

Katherine L. Gordon is an Ontario poet, publisher, judge and reviewer with many books, anthologies and co-operative works, some translated into other languages.   She believes that poets united have the power to transform life.

Heidi Greco lives in Surrey, BC, in a house surrounded by a very compact forest. In 2021 Anvil Books will publish her *Glorious Birds: A Celebratory Homage to Harold and Maude,* a book about one of her all-time favourite films. More info at heidigreco.ca

Elizabeth Greene, from Kingston, Ontario, has published three collections of poetry and a novel, *A Season Among Psychics.* She is the editor of *The Dowager Empress: Poems by Adele Wiseman* (Inanna, 2019).

Rosemary Griebel is a Calgary-based librarian and the author of *Yes* (Frontenac, 2011). In 2019 her poem "Walking with Walt Whitman Through Calgary's Eastside on a Winter Day" was selected for Project Bookmark's first Alberta literary landmark on the CanLit Trail.

Louise B. Halfe-Sky Dancer is a Cree poet, originally from Alberta, who served as Saskatchewan's Poet Laureate for two years. Her books of poetry have received numerous awards and she has been awarded honorary degrees by three universities. She lives near Saskatoon, Saskatchewan.

Vivian Hansen is a Calgary poet, whose publications include *Leylines of My Flesh* (Touchwood Press), *A Bitter Mood of Clouds*, and *A Tincture of Sunlight* (Frontenac House) She has work forthcoming in *(M)othering* (Inanna Press 2022), and *You Look Good For Your Age* (University of Alberta Press 2021).

Lea Harper is an award-winning poet and singer-songwriter; the author of two collections of poems, *All That Saves Us* and *Shadow Crossing* (Black Moss Press), and 4 recordings. She lives on a lake in Haliburton, Ontario, where she is completing her next book of poems and her first novel.

Maureen Hynes is a Toronto poet who has published five books of poetry, and whose poems have appeared in over 25 anthologies. Her most recent collection, *Sotto Voce,* was a finalist for the League of Canadian Poets' Pat Lowther Award, and the Golden Crown Literary Award (U.S.). www.maureenhynes.ca

Yasmin Ladha is a writer from Calgary who teaches in Muscat, Oman. Her more recent books are *Country Drive* (Red River) co-authored with Sukrita Paul and *Blue Sunflower Startle* (Freehand Books).

Donna Langevin is a Toronto poet, whose fifth poetry collection, *Brimming* was published by Piquant Press, 2019. Her play, *Summer of Saints* about the 1847 typhus epidemic during the Irish Potato Famine is scheduled to be produced by Act 2, Ryerson University, and published by Prometea Press in 2021.

John B. Lee is Poet Laureate of Norfolk County, the city of Brantford and the Canada Cuba Literary Alliance. His most recent book, Darling, may I touch your pinkletink, is published by Hidden Brook Press in 2020. He lives in Port Dover, Ontario.

Shelley A. Leedahl is the author of twelve books in various genres, including *The Moon Watched It All* (Red Deer Press) and *I Wasn't Always Like This* (Signature Editions). Leedahl has lived in all three western provinces and currently resides in Ladysmith on Vancouver Island, where she is an avid hiker and kayaker.

Josephine LoRe's words have been read on stage, put to music, danced, and integrated into visual art. She has two collections, Unity and The Cowichan Series (a Calgary Herald Bestseller) and has been published in anthologies and literary journals in nine countries including FreeFall Magazine and the Mount Fuji Tanka Grand Prix. In 2019, she was shortlisted for the Room Magazine Poetry Prize. https://www.josephinelorepoet.com/

Laurie MacFayden is an award-winning writer, painter and sports journalist from Ontario who has lived in Alberta for over 30 years. In addition to three poetry collections published by Frontenac House, her work has appeared in *The New Quarterly, Alberta Views, FreeFall, Queering The Way*; and been performed in Edmonton's Skirts Afire! Festival, Loud & Queer cabaret, and the Queer the Arts Festival in Calgary.

Alex Manley is a non-binary Canadian writer who's lived in Montreal/Tiohtià:ke their whole life. A graduate of Concordia University's creative writing program, their writing has been published by *Maisonneuve* magazine, The Puritan, Peach Mag, Carte Blanche, Powder Keg, *Grain, Vallum*, and the Academy of American Poets' Poem-a-Day feature, among others. Their debut poetry collection, *We Are All Just Animals & Plants*, was published by Metatron Press in 2016.

Diana Manole is a Romanian-born Canadian writer, translator, professor, and scholar, who currently lives in Toronto, Ontario. She has published nine collections of poems, short prose, and drama in her home country; her first poetry book in Canada, *Praying to a Landed-Immigrant God*, is forthcoming from Grey Borders Book in a bilingual Romanian-English edition.

Blaine Marchand has published six books of poetry, a young adult novel, a work of non-fiction and a chapbook. His work has been published in Canada, the US, Pakistan and New Zealand. His current manuscript, *Becoming History*, explores the life of his mother, who lived to almost 104. He lives in Ottawa, Ontario.

Katherine Matiko recently completed a short story collection, seeking inspiration from the seemingly unremarkable Calgary suburb where she has lived for the past 22 years. Several of her poems have been published, with a forthcoming appearance in the (M)othering Anthology with Inanna Publications.

Dr. Micheline Maylor is Calgary's Past Poet Laureate 2016-18. Her latest poetry collection, *The Bad Wife*, is due in 2021, and her previous is *Little Wildheart (U of Alberta Press, 2017)*.

Carley Mayson is a 29 year old poet who lives in Calgary, Alberta. She is dedicated to being very honest about experiences regarding mental health, the good along with the bad.

Rhona McAdam is the author of six full length poetry collections, the most recent of which are *Cartography* and *Ex-Ville*. She lives in Victoria.

Ray McGinnis is author of *Writing the Sacred: A Psalm-Inspired Path to Writing* and *Creating Sacred Poetry*. He lives in Vancouver, British Columbia, where he writes and walks from a distance.

Stuart Ian McKay is a Calgary poet. His work has been published in many Canadian literary journals and anthologies, most recently in even the idea of maya is maya, a poetry chapbook, by Frog Hollow Press(2019), as part of its Dis/ability series.

Pamela Medland is a Calgary poet whose work has appeared online and in print in numerous literary journals and anthologies. Pamela's elderly mother survived a COVID-19 outbreak in which nineteen residents and workers tested positive and three died.

Bruce Meyer is author or editor of 64 books of poetry, short fiction, flash fiction, and non-fiction. His most recent collection of poems is *McLuhan's Canary* (Guernica Editions, 2019). He lives in Barrie, Ontario, and teaches at Georgian College.

Anna Mioduchowska's poetry, poetry translations, stories, essays and book reviews have appeared in several anthologies and literary journals, and have aired on the CBC and CKUA Radio. She has published two poetry collections: *In-Between Season* and *Some Souls Do Well in Flowerpots*. She lives in Edmonton.

Colin Morton is an Ottawa poet who has published over a dozen books and chapbooks ranging from visual and sound poetry to historical narratives. His other work includes stories and reviews, a novel (*Oceans Apart*) and an animated film (*Primiti Too Taa*). www.colinmorton.net.

Erín Moure is a poet and translator of poetry based in Montréal. Her most recent translations are of Chantal Neveu's *This Radiant Life* (Book*hug, 2020), from French, and Uxío Novoneyra's *The Uplands: Book of the Courel and other poems* (Veliz Books, 2020) from Galician. Her own most recent book is *The Elements* (Anansi, 2019).

Sarah Xerar Murphy, an author with many books to her credit, won 2019's New Brunswick Book Awards Mrs Dunster's Fiction Prize for the first volume of her two volume novel *Itzel: A Tlatelolco Awakening*. The second volume *Itzel II: A Three Knives Tale* comes out in 2020. Sarah Xerar Murphy is also a performance, visual and spoken word artist, as well as interpreter, translator, and activist in the struggle for social justice.

Lisa Pasold is originally from Montreal and now lives in New Orleans, where she's been photographing flowers during quarantine. Her 2012 book of poetry, *Any Bright Horse,* was shortlisted for the Governor General's Award.

Amanda Perry is originally from Edmonton. She completed a PhD in Comparative Literature at New York University. She now writes and teaches in Montréal.

Roberta Rees is inspired in her writing by the geography of the Rocky Mountains where she grew up and the rhythms of her working class roots. A longtime resident of Calgary, Roberta has published three books, many essays, poems and stories, enjoys hanging out with friends and family, playing her guitar, singing, hiking, engaging in social/political activism.

Giovanna Riccio is a Toronto poet who has published 3 books of poetry. Her latest book is *Plastic's Republic: Featuring the Barbie Suite* published by Guernica Editions (2019).

Ellie Sawatzky (elliesawatzky.com) is a poet and writer from Kenora, Ontario, currently based in Vancouver. She was a poetry finalist for the 2019 Bronwen Wallace Award, and her début poetry collection is forthcoming from Nightwood Editions in Fall 2021.

Shirley A. Serviss is an Edmonton writer and writing instructor with three published poetry collections. She is the Staff Literary Artist on the Wards for the Friends of University Hospitals, but has been temporarily laid off due to the pandemic.

Christine Smart lives on Salt Spring Island, BC, the setting for her poem "Hummingbird" that won the 2020 Federation of BC Writers poetry contest. Hedgerow Press published two books of her poetry: *decked and dancing* (People's Poet Award 2007) and *The White Crow*.

Glen Sorestad is a much published poet from Saskatoon whose poems have appeared in over 25 books and chapbooks, over 70 anthologies and textbooks, and have been translated into at least eight languages. His latest book is the bilingual English/Italian *Selected Poems from Dancing Birches* (Impremix, Italy, 2020).

Carol A. Stephen writes in Carleton Place, Ontario, near Ottawa. Her poetry appears in Poetry Is Dead (May 2017), regional print journals, chapbooks anthologies and online.

Betsy Struthers is the author of nine books of poetry -- *Still* won the 2004 Pat Lowther Memorial Award -- three mystery novels, and a collection of short fiction. A past president of the League of Canadian Poets, she lives in Peterborough, Ontario.

Sandra Sugimoto was born and raised on the unceded lands of the Coast Salish peoples, specifically the Squamish, Musqueam and Tsleil-Waututh Nations in British Columbia. She is a third generation Japanese Canadian artist. Currently she is a student in the Writer's Studio at Simon Fraser University.

Fraser Sutherland is a poet, editor, and lexicographer who lives in Toronto. The most recent of his 18 books is the poetry collection *Bad Habits* (Mosaic, 2019*)*.

Laura Swart has taught creative and academic writing for over thirty years and is director of I-AM ESL, an international language school that uses story and song to teach the intricacies of English to refugees. Her novels, poetry, and plays are inspired by the Alberta Rocky Mountains, where she hikes, bikes, and lives with her husband.

Barb Thomas lives in Toronto. She is an educator, writer and facilitator, committed to promoting equity and democratic process in organizations. Her poems have been published in *Our Times,*, and in *Mourning has Broken: A Collection of Creative Writing about Grief and Healing.* Ed. Mara Koven, Liz Pearl.

Harry Thurston is a poet who lives in Tidnish Bridge, Nova Scotia. He is a Mentor in the Master of Fine Arts in Creative Nonfiction program, at University of King's College, Halifax.

Thomas Trofimuk is an Edmonton writer who has four novels out in the world (*The 52nd Poem, Doubting Yourself to the Bone, Waiting for Columbus,* and *This is All a Lie*) and is currently working on something called "The Forensics of Loss." He writes on an irregular basis for his own website; "writer, gardener, failed Buddhist" at www.thomastrofimuk.com and he is currently wearing a mask.

Debbie Ulrich, her husband Terry and their dog Beaker were in a bad car accident in 2002 making her a quadriplegic.

Terry Watada is a Toronto, Ontario, poet who has five poetry collections in print. His latest, "The Four Sufferings", was published by Mawenzi House Publishers (Toronto) in 2020.

Sheri-D Wilson D.Litt, C.M. (AB, BC) is the award-winning author of 13 books, 4 short films, and 4 albums which combine music and poetry. Poet Laureate Emeritus of Calgary (2018-2020), in 2019 Sheri-D was appointed one to the Order of Canada (for her contributions as a Spoken Word Poet and her leadership in the community), and in 2017 she received her Doctor of Letters— Honoris Causa from Kwantlen University. www.sheridwilson.com